THE **5**
ESSAYS

YOU MUST
MASTER TO BE
COLLEGE READY

FAMILIUS

Library of Congress Cataloging-in-Publication Data

LCCN: 2017941393

Print ISBN 9781945547188

Ebook ISBN 9781945547638

Printed in the United States of America

Edited by DeAnna Acker

Cover design by David Miles

Book design by Kurt Wahlner

Illustration licensed from Shutterstock

10 9 8 7 6 5 4 3 2 1

First Edition

THE 5 ESSAYS

YOU MUST MASTER TO BE COLLEGE READY

LAURA TORRES

CONTENTS

CHAPTER THREE

INTRODUCTION TO RESEARCH 70

CHAPTER FOUR

SUMMARY/RESPONSE ESSAYS 94

CHAPTER SEVEN
  WRITING PROMPTS

INTRODUCTION

Through my experience as an instructor of first-year college composition at several institutions, I became well aware of the range of ability and education that students bring with them from their secondary education. Those who have a background in writing different types of essays, along with solid research and argumentative skills, are well prepared for the college composition experience. Those who are not as prepared often lose confidence quickly as they play catch-up. This writing curriculum covers all of the essential writing skills that will help students enter college composition with confidence.

The book is divided into seven sections. There are five different essay types, and a section about research. The last section contains writing prompts for the Summary/Response, Research, and Argumentative Essays. Each essay section is broken into manageable steps that will help students develop a writing process that avoids the paralysis of staring at a blank page wondering where to start. Although each section is complete and stands alone, each builds on the last. The essay types follow a progression. For example, the Summary/Response essay is the perfect segue into the research paper. The skills from the research paper form the basis for the more advanced argumentative essay. Students should work through this book from beginning to end for maximum benefit.

FOR PARENTS

Each essay section is self-directed, but it is essential that students have parental involvement in setting a timeline and in revising and grading.

The first step is to go through the essay unit with your student and set a timeline. Write down due dates for each step on the provided assignment sheet. Keep in mind that the essays that require outside research will require plenty of time for research. Finding good sources can be the most time-consuming part of this type of essay.

During the process, you might want to help your student brainstorm ideas and check in as they complete each step of the process.

When your student has completed a first draft, he or she will need several readers to critique the essay. A critique sheet is provided to help readers spot issues for revision. Resist the urge to "correct" the essay, and make suggestions instead. The writing should be entirely the student's, not a transcription of your corrections.

A grading rubric is provided if you wish to give a numerical grade. The rubric should not be a surprise to the student, but rather a tool to guide the essay. The student should have the grading rubric during all stages of the process so that expectations are clear.

Remember to give positive feedback all along the way. In my experience, positive feedback is essential to a student's confidence and improvement.

FOR STUDENTS

Writing an essay can sometimes seem overwhelming, but each essay unit here is broken into manageable steps. When you take one step at a time, the process becomes much easier and writing a great essay can even be an enjoyable experience.

Resist the urge to skip the prewriting steps. Each step contains essential skills that lead to a successful essay. If you take the process step by step, you will find yourself prepared and organized to write the rough draft.

Don't be afraid to ask for help at any stage of the process. A fresh set of eyes on your ideas, your thesis, or a draft in progress can be immensely helpful.

Most importantly, be open to critiques and suggestions. No one, including professional writers, gets it right the first time. There is always room for improvement. The revision process is the most important step to a polished, successful essay.

No matter what course of study you choose to pursue in the future, critical thinking skills and the ability to communicate clearly and convincingly are fundamental. By working through these essay units, you will be prepared for the college experience and beyond.

Happy Writing!
Laura Torres

Visit my blog at:
http://www.compositionclassroom.blogspot.com
for more ideas and resources.

BEFORE YOU BEGIN

Although each type of essay is unique in its process and structure, there are a few things that they all have in common.

AUDIENCE AND PURPOSE

You should know two things before you begin an essay: your audience and your purpose.

Your audience is the people for whom the essay is intended. These are the people you would hope to persuade. Even if only a few people will actually read the essay, you need to have this audience in mind when making your writing choices.

For example, if you were writing an argumentative essay on the connection between fast food and childhood obesity, you would make different choices if the audience were parents than if the audience were fast food executives. If you were writing a narrative essay about the time you practiced hard to win a race, the way you tell the story might be different if your audience were classmates rather than your coach.

Once you determine your audience, then you should carefully consider your purpose. Are you primarily trying to educate your audience about an issue, persuade them to see your point of view, or even take action?

For academic essays, you are rarely simply relaying information or trying to entertain your audience. Essays are meant to communicate an opinion, an argument, or share a point of view through narrative. In other words, you are trying to persuade your audience to think, consider, or do something.

When you have the audience and purpose in mind, your essay will have a better focus. With this focus, the writing process will be much easier.

THE PROCESS

Each essay is a multi-step process. The worst way to write an essay is to sit down and start writing a complete draft. The writing process has many steps, and each step is important to the finished product.

The process for each essay will be different depending on the type, but they all have this in common: the most important step is revision. Multiple drafts are necessary to a successful finished essay. This is where the real work happens.

Revision is different from proofreading. Revision is when you rethink and rewrite the parts of your essay that could be better. Think about the ideas, structure, organization, clarity, and overall purpose. You should not be too concerned with fixing punctuation or small grammar issues in revision.

Here are some general steps for the revision process after you have completed a draft and had a few people critique the essay for you:

1. Review the critiques of your essay. Decide which comments you should consider. Remember that this is your paper, and you do not have to take every suggestion. Of course it makes sense to pay close attention to the same comments from more than one person.

2. Fill out the Next Step Worksheet.

3. Review the assignment sheet and the grading rubric to make sure you have met all the requirements.

4. Mark the places on the essay where you want to revise.

5. Rewrite your draft and print out a fresh copy.

6. Read your essay out loud to yourself, or ask someone to read it to you as you follow along. Listen for awkward sentences or errors in structure.

7. Now it's time to re-read the essay one last time and proof-read. This is where you correct any punctuation or other small grammar issues.

CHAPTER ONE

NARRATIVE ESSAYS

A narrative essay is a personal story with a purpose. It is written in first person ("I"), and it gives you an opportunity to share an experience from your own life when you gained insight or learned something. Narrative essays are fun to read because your message, or purpose, is conveyed through storytelling.

The three main components of a good narrative essay are:

1. Plot:

A narrative essay is, first and foremost, a story. Like any good story, it has characters, action, and a story arc.

2. Description:

Allowing your readers to experience the story through sensory detail, rather than by just telling them about it, is key to effective storytelling.

3. Purpose:

Just like any other type of essay, a narrative essay has a purpose. It may not be obviously stated, and your essay may not necessarily include a thesis statement, but your reader will come away with new understanding.

You can write about a simple, small moment or a dramatic episode; the important thing is that it means something to you.

SAMPLE STUDENT NARRATIVE ESSAY

Bailey Grayson

Torres

English 105

21 January 2017

Teaching an Old Dog New Tricks

Ever since I was a kid, I hated dogs. Everyone in my family was a cat person. My dad especially disliked the barking, annoying dogs in our neighborhood. Cats were clean, quiet, demanded little work, and did their business in a designated box filled with litter. Best of all, they didn't mind if you left them for a few days, as long as they had a supply of food and clean water.

Dogs, on the other hand, barked, slobbered, pooped wherever they wanted, and required daily walks. My best friend's dog, Linus, didn't help my impression of the canine species. He was a gigantic, bony thing who chased my friend as she tore around her deck on her Big Wheel. She laughed hysterically, but I cowered in the corner of the yard, certain she'd be eaten, or at best, pinned down and drooled on.

So when my family decided to get a rescue dog for my brother, not only was I surprised, but I vowed to have nothing to do with it. I put down the ground rules: I didn't want it in my room, I didn't want to see any poop on our front lawn, and it better never, ever slobber on me. I did go to the shelter to help pick out the dog, however, because I wanted to have a vote in the matter.

When we got to the "medium" size dog section of the shelter (at least my parents had enough sense to veto the "large" dog choices) the smell of ammonia and dog food filled the air, along with uncertain whimpers and growls. Some of the dogs jumped up with their front paws pressing against the cages, barking and lunging at us. Some stayed curled up, awakened from a nap by the noise, and simply looked at us with sleepy eyes. My brother chose his dog, a caramel and black mutt with half-floppy ears, and deep chocolate eyes. She sat at my brother's feet and seemed to smile while he petted her, and gladly ran after a rope toy when he threw it. She obeyed commands to sit and stay, which made me like her a little bit; plus, her tail never stopped wagging. I had to smile when my brother dubbed her "Snickers" for the candy bar she resembled. Still, when my parents filled out the papers and loaded her into the car, I had my doubts. Dogs were the enemy, and now one would be invading my home, perhaps chewing up my shoes and my favorite sweater.

A few weeks into dog ownership, I'd surprised myself by asking to take her with me on my daily run, because it made the time go by so much faster to have such an enthusiastic companion.

I even found myself slipping her a piece of steak under the table, clearly against rules. Even my dog-averse parents seemed to like to have her around. Then one day, I was alone in the house when a terrible smell wafted into the room. Sure enough, when I went to investigate, there it was, in the middle of the carpet.

"Snickers!" I screeched.

She came into the room, tail between her legs, ears flat against the side of her face. Her head hung down, and she plopped down at my feet. She looked up at me with eyes that said she knew she'd done something wrong. She followed me as I opened all the windows, putting her head on my foot every time I paused. Something in me shifted. I knew she hadn't meant to make a mess. When I was all done, she curled up next to me in the other room, looked up at me, and wagged her tail.

"It's all right, Snickers," I said. "I know you didn't mean to do it." Who would have thought it was possible that I would be comforting this creature after cleaning up its mess? "Let's go for a walk, Snickers," I said. She twirled in circles and I felt my own heart twirl, too, just a little.

ESSAY ASSIGNMENT

Write a 1 1/2 page, typed, double-spaced narrative essay. Choose a story that fits the scope of the essay and has a purpose. Remember to include concrete, or sensory, details.

The grading criteria is as follows:

Purpose/Thesis: 25 points

The essay has a clear purpose. The thesis is clearly stated or implied.

Story and Structure: 20 points

The essay contains a well-focused, engaging, forward-moving story.

It is clearly a narrative essay and is the appropriate length.

Details: 15 points

The essay contains concrete details and avoids unnecessary abstractions.

Conventions: 15 points

The essay contains few grammatical and punctuation errors.

Total: 75 points

PREWRITING TECHNIQUES

Prewriting techniques are meant to help you get warmed up and start a free flow of ideas. There is no wrong or right, just a free flow of ideas.

Each of the following exercises has a time limit. The reason is that you should work quickly and spontaneously, and not overthink each topic. No idea is too silly to write down. The point is to keep the ideas flowing.

BRAINSTORMING LIST

Set a timer for two minutes and list as many ideas as you can for a personal narrative essay. Remember that this is a story that is meaningful to you and could be told in a short amount of time.

Name: _____

1. _____

2. _____

3. _____

4. _____

5. _____

6. _____

7. _____

8. _____

9. _____

10. _____

CLUSTERING

Choose two topics from your brainstorming session. Write your first topic in the circle in the middle of the paper. Set a timer for two minutes and make clusters of related ideas. Think of ideas that relate to the topic and draw them in connecting circles. Now continue, and draw your own circles and connecting lines. Your cluster can go in all different directions.

In the example, you can see that the student started with "Getting a dog" and branched off to different ideas.

Do a second cluster the same way with another topic. Circle a section of one of the clusters that interests you the most.

EXAMPLE CLUSTER:

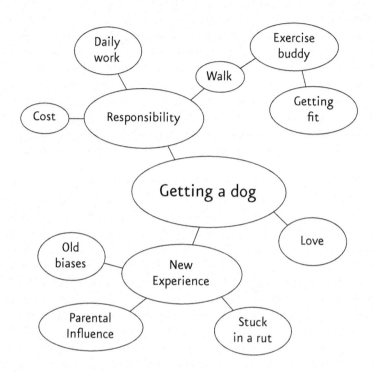

CLUSTER #1

Name: _____

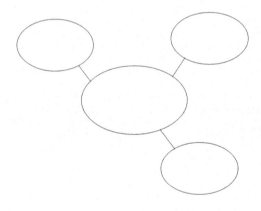

CLUSTER #2

Name: _____

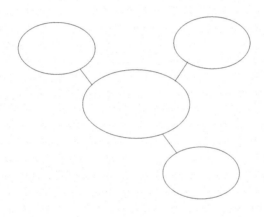

FREE WRITING

When free writing, you should never stop writing, even if you run out of things to say about the topic. If this happens, just write something such as, "I can't think of what to write next . . ." Spelling, punctuation, and grammar aren't important for these exercises.

FREE WRITE #1

Name: _____

Set a timer for three minutes to write as much as you can on the ideas you circled on one of your clusters.

FREE WRITE #2

Name: _____

Re-read your first free write. Circle the most interesting idea. When the time starts for this free write, start with this idea and continue writing until the end of the time period. If time allows, do the same thing for another round.

DECIDING ON A STORY

After you've done your free writing and you have a few ideas for your essay, it's time to choose your story. Write down your three best ideas here:

1. _____

2. _____

3. _____

For each of these ideas, ask yourself the following questions:

1. **Can I tell this story in 1 1/2 pages?**
   You need to be sure that your story isn't too long or too complicated for the amount of space allowed. This is called the scope of the story. It's best to limit your story to one simple episode that lends itself to good description.

2. **Did I learn something or gain insight from this experience?**
   Since your story will need to have a purpose, the first step is to think about whether you learned something or gained some sort of new understanding. Although the purpose does not need to be anything life-changing (in fact, sometimes a small insight is better), you need to make sure your story has the potential for a purpose.

3. **Is this topic appropriate to share?** This assignment contains a personal story, but remember that it is meant to be read by others. Be sure you are comfortable having an audience for this story.

After you've gone through all the questions, circle the choice that seems to fit the assignment best. You've got your story!

OUTLINING THE STORY

Although telling a personal story might seem simple because no one knows what happened better than you, it's easy to go off on a tangent. A tangent is something that happened or something you want to explain that isn't important to the story.

For example, if your story is about how a cake you baked for your aunt fell apart in the car on the way over to her birthday party, you might be tempted to tell about the time your uncle won a pie-eating contest, because thinking about your aunt reminds you of your uncle. Resist the urge. Stick to the main story, or your reader will become confused or distracted. Use the graphic planner to keep your story on track. Also, list some details that you might want to describe to help you decide which are the most important.

EXAMPLE NARRATIVE ESSAY PLANNER

> Introduction—
> What do we need to know?
>
> My history of disliking dogs — family, best friend's dog Linus, why I liked cats

Choose a few things to describe—an emotion, an object, something that you see, taste, smell, or experience.

> Rising Action
>
> Family deciding to get brother a dog, going to the pound, picking one out and bringing it home. I start to take her on runs and feed her under the table.

> What should I describe?
> Friend's dog Linus

> What should I describe?
> The pound - smell, dogs

> Climax
>
> I'm home alone with the dog and it poops on the carpet. I get mad and have to clean it up and yell at the dog.

> What should I describe?
> Description of the dog my brother chose

> Falling Action
>
> I can tell the dog feels bad and I end up comforting the dog and feeling bad for her.

> What should I describe?
> How the dog reacted when I yelled at her

> Resolution/Conclusion
>
> I decide to take the dog for a run and feel almost as excited as she is. Who knew? I surprised myself by liking the dog.

> What should I describe?
> How I felt when she was excited to go for a run

NARRATIVE ESSAY PLANNER

Introduction—
What do we need to know?

Choose a few things to describe—an emotion, an object, something that you see, taste, smell, or experience.

Rising Action

What should I describe?

What should I describe?

Climax

What should I describe?

Falling Action

What should I describe?

Resolution/Conclusion

What should I describe?

DISCOVERING YOUR PURPOSE

Once you've got your story outline, it's time to consider the purpose of the story. You do not want to be preachy or hit your reader over the head with a purpose (You should be kind to animals! Animals are helpless creatures!), but your purpose should be clear to the reader through the story.

See if you can answer these questions about the purpose of your essay:

1. What specific thing did I learn from this experience?

_____

2. What could someone else take away from this essay, even if they haven't had the same experience?

_____

Here's how these questions would be answered for the sample essay:

1. What specific thing did I learn from this experience?

I learned that I didn't really hate dogs. I just didn't have enough experience to know the good side of dog ownership, or how much I could love a dog.

2. What could someone else take away from this essay, even if they haven't had the same experience?

You shouldn't judge whether you like something or not based on others' opinions or limited experience. Keep an open mind and great things could happen. Old dogs can learn new tricks!

If you've answered these questions, you've got your purpose. Now your job is to be sure you show your readers through your story and not just tell them. Try to work the purpose into the body of the story; it's usually best to revisit the purpose in the conclusion as well.

The purpose of the sample essay was to show that you shouldn't judge whether you like something or not based on others' opinions or on limited experience. Here's how the writer of the sample essay worked the purpose into the conclusion:

> "It's all right, Snickers," I said. "I know you didn't mean to do it." Who would have thought it was possible that I would be comforting this creature after cleaning up its mess? "Let's go for a walk, Snickers," I said. She twirled in circles and I felt my own heart twirl, too, just a little.

The writer didn't say, "I guess I like dogs after all, and therefore, you shouldn't judge whether you like something or not until you try it." Instead, she showed the lesson by describing how she felt at the end of the story. "I felt my own heart twirl, too," shows that she felt excited to be with the dog. "Who would have thought it was possible that I would be comforting this creature after cleaning up its mess?" shows that she feels compassion for the dog and is beginning to see that the good outweighs the bad. This type of showing allows the readers to discover the meaning for themselves, which is much more effective than preaching a lesson to them.

EFFECTIVE DESCRIPTION

What is the difference between these two paragraphs?

Paragraph #1

> I was really scared to ride the roller coaster. I
> felt a little sick, but excited at the same time.
> When the bar clicked into place, I held on tight.
> When the ride started, I hoped for the best.

Paragraph #2

> As I slid into the red plastic seat of the roller
> coaster, my mouth went dry and my hands
> felt clammy. The bar in front of me clicked
> into place and I gripped it so hard my knuckles
> turned white. I could taste the cotton candy
> I'd eaten earlier at the back of my throat.
> When the car jolted forward, my stomach
> dropped, I held my breath, and I told myself I
> would survive.

In the first paragraph, the writer is *telling* the reader what is happening. In the second paragraph, the writer is *showing* the reader, or putting the reader in the story, allowing him or her to experience what the writer experienced. The writer accomplishes this through concrete, or sensory, detail.

Words like "scared" or "excited" tell an emotion, but don't show it. These are abstract descriptions, because there's nothing to see, hear, feel, taste, or smell. In the second example, the reader experiences "scared" when the writer says, "my mouth went dry and my hands felt clammy." The reader understands that the writer "felt a little sick" when the writer says, "I could taste the cotton candy I'd eaten earlier in the back of my throat." The reader feels the anxiety when the writer says, "I gripped it so hard my knuckles turned white." This is showing, rather than telling.

> **TIP**
>
> You don't have to describe everything. Just a few concrete descriptions go a long way!

Following are three writing picture prompts to help you practice writing concrete detail.

PICTURE PROMPT #1

Use concrete detail to show what it would be like to be this bike racer. What does he see? What does he hear? What is he thinking? What is going on inside his body? Use all the senses to help the reader be in the moment.

PICTURE PROMPT #2

Use concrete detail to describe what this man is feeling. What does he see? What does he hear? What is he thinking? Describe the emotion he is feeling.

PICTURE PROMPT #3

Use concrete detail to describe the setting as if you were here. What do you hear? What do you see? What do you smell? What does it feel like? Put the reader in the moment with you.

ROUGH DRAFT

Now that you have an outline, a purpose, and have practiced writing concrete detail, you are ready to write a draft. This draft is meant to be a starting place, so don't worry about getting everything perfect. You will have plenty of time to revise and make improvements later.

After you have written the rough draft, follow these steps for revision:

1. Use the Description Revision Worksheet to help revise the details in your essay.

2. Get at least two people to read your rough draft and critique it using the Narrative Essay Critique Worksheet.

3. Complete the Next Step Worksheet.

After completing these steps, it is helpful to write another draft, revise, proofread, and then write your final draft.

DESCRIPTION REVISION WORKSHEET

Name: _____

Find some examples of telling, rather than showing, in your essay. Then try and rewrite the abstract description so it uses concrete detail instead.

Example:

Abstract: *It smelled weird in the dog shelter and the dogs seemed to be nervous.*

Concrete: *The smell of ammonia and dog food filled the air, along with uncertain whimpers and growls.*

Abstract: _____ Concrete: _____
_____ _____
_____ _____

Abstract: _____ Concrete: _____
_____ _____
_____ _____

Abstract: _____ Concrete: _____
_____ _____
_____ _____

Abstract: _____ Concrete: _____
_____ _____
_____ _____

Abstract: _____ Concrete: _____
_____ _____
_____ _____

NARRATIVE ESSAY CRITIQUE

Your Name: _____

Author's Name: _____

1. What is the purpose of the essay?

2. Where do you find the purpose? Is it too obvious? Not obvious enough?

3. What is working well? List at least two things.

4. Is the essay appropriate for sharing? List at least one reason why or why not.

5. Is the scope of the essay appropriate for 1 1/2 pages? List at least one reason why or why not.

6. Underline concrete details. Circle details that are vague or abstract.

7. On the draft, mark any passages that are confusing to you or don't make sense.

8. On the draft, mark any passages that don't move the story forward (tangents).

9. Is the conclusion satisfying and effective? List at least one reason why or why not.

10. List any other suggestions for the author.

NEXT STEP WORKSHEET

Name: _____

What are three things I learned about my essay from my
   critiques?

   1. _____

   2. _____

   3. _____

What two things do I need to do next to improve my essay?
   (List more if desired.)

   1. _____

   2. _____

NARRATIVE GRADING RUBRIC

Purpose   /25 points

The essay has a clear purpose. It is clearly
stated or implied.

Story and Structure   /20 points

The essay contains a well-focused, engaging,
forward-moving story.
It is clearly a narrative essay and is the
appropriate length.

Details   /15 points

The essay contains concrete details and
avoids unnecessary abstractions.

Conventions   /15 points

The essay contains few grammatical and
punctuation errors.

_____

75 points total

Comments:

CHAPTER TWO

COMPARE/CONTRAST ESSAYS

The compare/contrast essay is an exercise in critical thinking and organization. While the narrative essay was a personal experience, likely organized chronologically, the compare/contrast essay will help you to look objectively at two ideas, form an opinion, and present it in an organized way. Outlining is particularly important for this type of essay to stay organized.

SAMPLE STUDENT COMPARISON ESSAY
(POINT-BY-POINT FORMAT)

Olivia Senter

Torres

English 155

15 January 2016

"The Raven" and "The Black Cat" by Edgar Allan Poe

To say that Edgar Allan Poe had a dark view of the world around him would be stating the obvious. Poe lived a life that was wrought with tragedy and pain. His two stories "The Raven" and "The Black Cat" are good examples of the themes that run through his work of superstition, judgment, sorrow, and retribution, all showing the darkness in his own life.

The two stories both play on the superstitions of black animals and their evil representations. In "The Black Cat," the idea of this superstition is brought up by the protagonist's wife's references to "the ancient popular notion, which regarded all black cats as witches in disguise." "The Raven," on the other hand, sits in judgment of the narrator from above the doorway. As he sits imagining why this messenger should appear at his door, he starts thinking the superstitious belief that this raven is somehow his departed love, Lenore.

Judgment is a constant in both stories, as both protagonists feel they are constantly being sized up for their actions. In "The Black Cat," the cat is always at his side, never leaving him alone, unaware of the violence that bubbles beneath his surface. His wife, an always agreeable and non-confrontational companion, makes him question whether he deserves someone so good. He perceives the second cat, more cloying in its attention and devotion than the first one, as killing him with kindness. It's as if he is being reminded of how bad he is by the goodness that surrounds him, and it's mocking him in his alcohol-riddled mind. He even goes so far as to rationalize his dealings of death as if they were the most common of occurrences in everyone's daily life. "The Raven," in comparison, sits perched above the door looking down upon the narrator with no emotion at all, and in his half-awake mind, the narrator wonders what the meaning behind its arrival could signify. Is it his long-lost love, coming to mock him and his loneliness, or is the raven simply the dark judgment he feels within himself as he sits alone?

Both stories have strong elements of sorrow. In "The Black Cat" the reader feels that the protagonist is sorrowful, not for the heinous actions he commits, but more for the eventual lack of companionship and how that affects him at that moment. He is deeply introverted and only reacts to what is affecting him, not giving much thought to the effects of his behavior on the people and things around him. "The Raven" is more of a sorrow for a lost love, which is a very strong current that runs in most of Poe's work, as his real life was wrought with loss and sorrow from a very young age.

Retribution for wrongs committed has a strong foothold in "The Black Cat" and "The Raven." The darkness, or evil, is a constant undercurrent in these two stories, with animals sitting as judge and jury over the protagonists in their minds. There must be a price to pay for these evil thoughts and actions, and who is the punisher at the end of the day, himself or the evil he is so wrapped up in? Poe references Pluto, the Greek god of the underworld and "Plutonian shore," a reference to Hell and Hades, in both stories. He rationalizes that every man has evil thoughts. He tries to make light of the evil actions that go along with those thoughts, as if everyone acts upon them as he has.

Both stories were dark and intense but also unique in their approach to the darkness. "The Black Cat" was more about the evil that man can think and act upon with the aid of intoxication, and "The Raven" was more about the sorrow and judgment of lost love and wonder about the afterlife. Evil is always a counterbalance to the good in life and when that balance shifts too far one way, madness is not far to follow. Unfortunately for Poe, these themes were also currents in his own life.

COMPARE/CONTRAST ESSAY ASSIGNMENT

Write a compare/contrast essay, at least 1 ½ pages long, **using the point-by-point, block, or combo method.**

- The first paragraph should include an introduction and your thesis statement.

- Each body paragraph should begin with a topic sentence, and the final paragraph should be the conclusion (not just a restatement of the thesis).

The grading criteria is as follows:

Thesis: 25 points
   The essay has a clear opinion in the thesis statement.

Organization: 25 points
   The essay is organized in point-by-point or block or combo format.

Topic Sentences: 20 points
   The essay contains clear topic sentences that support the thesis.

Introduction/Conclusion: 15 points
   The introduction and conclusion are engaging.

Conventions: 15 points
   The essay contains few grammatical and punctuation errors.

Total: 100 points

COMPARE/CONTRAST ESSAY TOPICS

A compare/contrast essay is often used at the elementary level to point out the differences and similarities between two physical objects. The more sophisticated compare/contrast essay focuses on ideas and more scholarly topics, such as similar themes in two short stories, or the differences between two career choices. Usually an essay of this type also concentrates primarily on either comparing to show similarities, or contrasting to show differences between the two topics. The first step is to decide on a topic. Below are a few broad ideas to get you started:

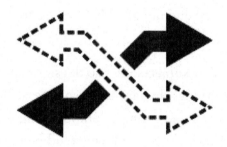

- movie versus book
- career choices
- college choices
- poets or works of poetry
- short stories
- works of art
- consumer products

NARROWING YOUR TOPIC

Once you have a broad topic, the next step is to narrow it down to something you can write about effectively in an essay. Here are some guidelines:

1. **Be specific:** It doesn't make sense to write about a topic that is too broad, such as the differences between living in Hawaii and living in Alaska. Most people can easily imagine the differences, so your essay won't be compelling to your audience. A better topic, for example, would be the difference in costs between living in Hawaii and living in Alaska. This is specific and not already obvious, so it's more likely to be interesting.

2. **Choose similar subjects:** It also doesn't make sense to choose two things that are too disparate, such as a career choice between becoming a computer engineer or becoming a lawyer. A more logical choice would be to compare going into network security versus software development, or deciding between family law and criminal law.

NARROWING YOUR TOPIC WORKSHEET

Write down a few topic ideas here and then some possible similar, specific subject ideas:

Name: _____

Topic: _____

Subjects: _____ _____

Subjects: _____ _____

Subjects: _____ _____

Topic: _____

Subjects: _____ _____

Subjects: _____ _____

Subjects: _____ _____

Topic: _____

Subjects: _____ _____

Subjects: _____ _____

Subjects: _____ _____

Now circle your favorite idea from this page and start your essay prewriting using the Venn diagram worksheet. The Venn diagram helps you brainstorm the differences and similarities in your topic. Label each circle with each thing you are comparing and contrasting. The unique characteristics go in the outer circles. The similarities go in the intersection.

PREWRITING TECHNIQUES

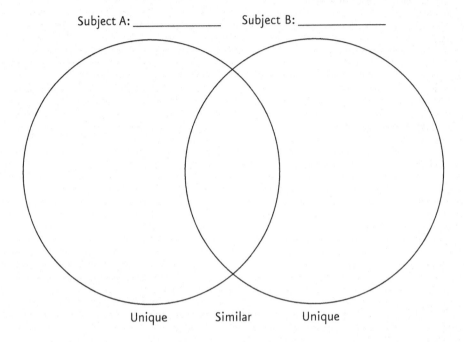

Subject A: _____   Subject B: _____

Unique   Similar   Unique

Circle the three most important differences for each topic, then circle the three most important similarities.

Decide whether your essay would be better primarily showing the similarities (compare essay) or primarily showing the differences (contrast essay).

THE THESIS STATEMENT

A compare and contrast essay shouldn't have a surprise ending. In other words, be sure to state your opinion clearly in the thesis statement. If you don't state your opinion, you risk a ho-hum thesis. Notice the difference between these two thesis statements:

Thesis #1

There are many differences between organic food and conventional food.

Thesis #2

Organic food is superior to conventional food.

The second thesis is better, but it is still a bit of a "so what?" thesis. Why might your opinion be important to your audience? Consider how this thesis statement might resonate better with a wider audience:

Organic food is better for you than conventional food.

To keep your essay organized and focused, it's best to list from two to four points of argument in your thesis.

Organic food is superior to conventional food because of its nutrition and safety.

Finally, if it makes sense, you can work in a reference to the similarities if it's a contrast essay, or a difference if it's a compare essay. In other words, mention the opposite point so the reader can see you have carefully analyzed the topic.

Contrast Essay:

Although similar in taste [similarity], organic food is superior to conventional food because of its nutrition and safety.

Compare Essay:

Organic food is superior to conventional food because of its nutrition and safety; **although it can be more expensive** [difference], the benefits are worth the extra cost.

Create your own "working thesis" (called this because it can change through the writing process), on the worksheet for either a primarily comparison essay or a primarily contrast essay, then organize your ideas using one of the outlining methods: block, point-by-point, or combo organization.

DEVELoPING A THESIS STATEMENT FOR A CONTRAST ESSAY

What is your opinion on the subject?

_____

Which three differences inform this opinion the best?

1. _____

2. _____

3. _____

What are the most important similarities?

1. _____

2. _____

Working thesis:

_____

_____

DEVELoPING A THESIS STATEMENT FOR A COMPARISoN ESSAY

What is your opinion on the subject?

_____

Which three differences inform this opinion the best?

1. _____

2. _____

3. _____

What are the most important similarities?

1. _____

2. _____

Working thesis:

_____

_____

POINT-BY-POINT ORGANIZATION

The point-by-point method of organization works well when the subjects you are comparing and contrasting could benefit from discussing details side-by-side rather than separately. If your subjects have subtle differences, this might be the best choice.

POINT-BY-POINT EXAMPLE OUTLINE

Thesis statement: Edgar Allan Poe's "The Raven" and "The Black Cat" have themes of superstition, sorrow, and judgment.

Point A: Superstition

Subject 1. "The Raven"

Subject 2. "The Black Cat"

Point B: Sorrow

Subject 1. "The Raven"

Subject 2. "The Black Cat"

Point C: Judgment

Subject 1. "The Raven"

Subject 2. "The Black Cat"

Conclusion

POINT-BY-POINT OUTLINE

Name: _____

Thesis statement:

_____

_____

Point A:

    Subject 1.

    Subject 2.

Point B:

    Subject 1.

    Subject 2.

Point C:

    Subject 1.

    Subject 2.

Conclusion

BLOCK ORGANIZATION

The block method is a good choice when you think your subjects are best dealt with separately. If they are very different, or easily confused, the block method can help keep things clear.

EXAMPLE BLOCK OUTLINE

Thesis statement: Although working as a nurse in any capacity requires superior people skills, working in an emergency room rather than a doctor's office requires someone who has specialized trauma training, works well under pressure, and doesn't mind variable hours.

Subject 1: Emergency room nurse

Point A. Training

Point B. Pressure

Point C. Hours

Subject 2: Doctor's office nurse

Point A. Training

Point B. Pressure

Point C. Hours

Conclusion

BLOCK OUTLINE

Name: _____

Thesis statement:

_____

_____

Point A:

    Subject 1.

    Subject 2.

Point B:

    Subject 1.

    Subject 2.

Point C:

    Subject 1.

    Subject 2.

Conclusion

COMBO ORGANIZATION

Sometimes the point-by-point or block methods can seem a bit simplistic. As long as you can stay focused and keep your arguments clear, you might want to try a combination of the two methods. A good starting point for an organization of this type is to use a few paragraphs of the block method, then end with a paragraph of point-by-point.

COMBO EXAMPLE OUTLINE

Thesis statement: Organic food is superior to conventional food because of its nutrition and safety; although it can be more expensive, the benefits are worth the extra cost.

Subject 1: Organic

Point A. Nutrition

Point B. Safety

Subject 2: Conventional

Point A. Nutrition

Point B. Safety

Point C. Price

Subject 1: Organic

Subject 2: Conventional

Conclusion

COMBO OUTLINE

Name: _____

Thesis statement:

_____

_____

Subject 1:

    Point A.

    Point B.

Subject 2:

    Point A.

    Point B.

Point C:

    Subject 1.

    Subject 2.

Conclusion

INTRODUCTIONS AND CONCLUSIONS

INTRODUCTIONS

An introduction is not the same thing as a thesis statement. For a compare/contrast essay, the introduction serves to answer the "so what?" question. Why is this topic relevant? What can the reader learn? What new perspective can you offer?

Here are a few suggestions for effective introductions, using this thesis as an example:

> Organic food is superior to conventional food because of its nutrition and safety; although it can be more expensive, the benefits are worth the extra cost.

1. **Ask a question:** Fruits and vegetables are staples in a healthy diet, but what damaging chemicals could be lurking in that innocent-looking apple?

2. **Tell a story:** I was skeptical when a nutritionist recommended eating organic foods to see if they helped with my food sensitivities, but I began to have more energy and overall better health almost right away.

3. **Give an interesting fact or statistic:** Although some may think the label "organic" means pesticide-free, that is not necessarily the case.

4. **Illustrate a point with description:** It's easy to ignore where our food comes from, but the next time chicken is on the menu, consider the plight of animals who never set foot outside and spend all their lives in a small cage, and whose feed might contain antibiotics and animal products. Now consider chickens with access to the outdoors and certified organic feed. Which industry would you rather support?

5. **Give a reason why the topic is important to you:** My mother grew up on a farm and was regularly exposed to pesticides. She and her eight siblings all have health problems that could be related to this pesticide exposure.

Once you have hooked your reader with your introduction, then your thesis statement will state your argument.

CONCLUSIONS

It is tempting to simply restate your thesis instead of writing a satisfying conclusion. A summary of the main points can be helpful, especially if your essay is long, but your conclusion should be more than a repeat to be effective.

Here are a few ideas for starting your conclusions, using the same topic as above.

1. **Answer a question posed in the introduction or elsewhere in the essay:** That apple you ate for lunch likely contains residue of diphenylamine, a growth regulator, and several pesticides.

2. **Revisit a story told in the introduction:** Although there is no proof that my mother's and her siblings' health problems were directly caused by pesticides, the evidence suggests that they are almost certainly related.

3. **Propose a call to action:** The public should be aware of the differences between organic and conventional foods through mandated labeling in order to make more informed decisions.

4. **Give an anecdote or brief example:** The difference in cost between an organic apple and a conventional apple might be a quarter, but that extra quarter is money well spent.

ROUGH DRAFT

Now it's time to write a rough draft. A compare/contrast rough draft should simply flesh out your prepared outline.

After you have written the rough draft, follow these steps for revision:

1. Get at least two people to read your rough draft and critique it, using the Compare/Contrast Essay Critique worksheet.

2. Complete the Next Step worksheet.

After completing these steps, it is helpful to write another draft, revise, proofread, and then write your final draft.

COMPARE/CONTRAST ESSAY CRITIQUE

Your Name: _____

Author's Name: _____

1. What are the two elements being compared and contrasted?

2. What is the author's opinion? Underline where you find this on the draft. Does it appear in the thesis statement?

3. Identify and underline the topic sentence of each paragraph. Does each topic sentence introduce what will be addressed in the rest of the paragraph?

4. Does the essay follow the structure of a block, point-by-point, or combination format?

5. Does the author effectively compare or contrast the two elements?

6. Does the essay contain enough personal information or opinion to make it interesting? Identify any place the author could add more.

7. Suggestions and comments:

NEXT STEP WORKSHEET

Name: _____

What are three things I learned about my essay from my
   critiques?

   1. _____

   2. _____

   3. _____

What two things do I need to do next to improve my essay?
   (List more if desired.)

   1. _____

   2. _____

COMPARE/CONTRAST GRADING RUBRIC

Purpose/Thesis   /25 points

The essay has a clear opinion in the thesis statement.

Organization   /25 points

The essay is organized in point-by-point, block, or combo format.

Topic Sentences   /20 points

The essay contains clear topic sentences that support the thesis.

Introduction/Conclusion   /15 points

The introduction and conclusion are engaging.

Conventions   /15 points

The essay contains few grammatical and punctuation errors.

_____

100 points total

Comments:

CHAPTER THREE

INTRODUCTION TO RESEARCH

Most essays that you write on the secondary and college level will require research. Along with research comes a host of rules and guidelines for sources, citations, and formatting. These can seem overwhelming, but they are important and easily mastered by following the guidelines in the next three sections.

ACADEMIC SOURCES

What kind of sources can I use?

The best sources are peer reviewed. This means that an article or book was written by an expert in the field, and reviewed for accuracy by other experts. You will find peer reviewed articles in scholarly journals. Respected newspapers and magazines are also good sources.

Avoid blogs, personal websites, or work that has not been reviewed or edited, or any information which has uncertain origins. A source should not have an agenda or bias. Avoid sources trying to sell a product or promote a certain idea.

Primary sources are good as well. These are interviews that you conduct, surveys, personal experience, or observation. Laws, historical documents, and raw data are also primary sources.

Where do I find sources?

- **Academic search engines.** Many schools and libraries subscribe to academic search engines such as EBSCO or Academic Search Premiere or InfoTrac. These search engines filter results so you only get academic sources that you can be sure are appropriate sources.

- **Scholar.google.com.** This search engine, available to anyone, also filters results so you only get academic sources. Not every source listed is available online.

- **Library.** Print sources from your school or public library that you can't get online are available here. A librarian is a great resource. Ask him or her for help.

- **Internet search.** Using a regular search engine such as Google or Yahoo can turn up appropriate sources, but you have to be very careful to make sure your source is appropriate for an academic research paper.

What about Wikipedia?

Wikipedia is not a reliable or credible academic source. If you go to the end of an article on Wikipedia, however, you will find links that could lead you to an academic source.

AVOIDING PLAGIARISM

Plagiarism is the use of another person's words or ideas without crediting the source. It is a serious breach of academic honesty. At the very least, you will fail the assignment, and sometimes the consequences are much more severe. Even if you don't get caught, you have let yourself down by being dishonest and missing the opportunity to learn.

An example of plagiarism is to use someone else's paper as your own, or to directly copy information from a website or other source. You also need to avoid unintentional plagiarism, where you incorrectly use someone else's ideas simply because you don't know how to cite them properly. Ignorance of what constitutes plagiarism, however, is no excuse. The following guidelines will help you avoid making a mistake.

Example Source

"As one might imagine, Stegner was not in favor of the American Dream, or at least not the materialistic dream of status and possessions."

Benson, Jackson. *Wallace Stegner: His Life and Work*. New York: Viking, 1996.

Direct Quotation

If you use the exact words from a source, always use quotation marks, followed by a citation.

Correct: "As one might imagine, Stegner was not in favor of the American Dream, or at least not the materialistic dream of status and possessions" (Benson 10).

Plagiarized: As one might imagine, Stegner was not in favor of the American Dream, or at least not the materialistic dream of status and possessions. *(Missing quotation marks and citation)*

Paraphrase

If you use someone's idea, but do not use the exact words, you must still credit the source and include a citation. In addition, you cannot just change a few words; you must put the idea completely in your own words.

Correct: Wallace Stegner did not believe people should buy into the materialistic part of the American Dream (Benson 10).

Plagiarized: Wallace Stegner did not believe people should buy into the materialistic part of the American Dream. *(missing citation)*

Plagiarized: Wallace Stegner was not a fan of the American Dream, at least not the dream of status and possessions. *(only a few words changed, missing citation)*

Tips

- Resist the temptation to cut and paste from websites. Take notes in your own words instead, and use quotation marks or highlight direct quotations in your notes.

- Use multiple credible sources so all your information does not come from one place. When you synthesize ideas from many sources, you are more likely to understand the subject and be able to come up with your own ideas.

- If you are not sure if you are plagiarizing, go back and read the original source. If the ideas or words belong to someone else, cite them.

Combining Direct Quotes with Paraphrase

Correct: Wallace Stegner did not approve of the American Dream, or, as Benson said, "at least not the materialistic dream of status and possessions" (10).

Plagiarized: Wallace Stegner did not approve of the American Dream, or at least not the materialistic dream of status and possessions (Benson 10). *(using the author's own words without quotation marks)*

Common Knowledge

If a fact is common knowledge, meaning you can find the same information in multiple credible sources, it is something that most people already know, you observed it directly, or it is a generally accepted fact, you do not need to cite a source. Using the example above, if you have read several of Wallace Stegner's books yourself, you could say, without quotes or a citation, that his books are often critical of people with materialistic values. As another example, you could say that smoking is bad for your health without citing a source.

If you are not sure if something needs a citation, remember this rule: When in doubt, it's best to cite.

AVoiDING PLAGIARISM WORKSHEET

Below is original source material about secondhand smoke, followed by a student-written passage about the topic. Circle or highlight anywhere that you find plagiarism in the student passage.

Source:

A federally funded study has found that inhaling secondhand smoke affects the brain in much the same way as smoking a cigarette does. We've long known that people who smoke cigarettes put more than their own health at jeopardy. The Centers for Disease Control and Prevention estimates that secondhand smoke kills about 50,000 Americans each year. Exposure to secondhand smoke also increases the likelihood that children will start smoking cigarettes when they become teenagers and makes it harder for adult smokers to quit.

Miller, Michael, editor. "Secondhand Smoke and the Brain." *Harvard Mental Health Letter*, vol. 28, no. 3, 2011, EBSCO, http://www.health.harvard.edu/newsletter_article/secondhand-smoke-and-the-brain.

Student Passage:

Everyone knows that smoking is bad for your health, and studies have shown that secondhand smoke isn't good for you either. About 50,000 Americans every year are killed by secondhand smoke, according to the Centers for Disease Control and Prevention (Miller 7). In addition, a recent study has found that inhaling secondhand smoke affects the brain in much the same was as smoking a cigarette does. That means if you smoke around your child, the smoke may be affecting your child's brain as much as your own. Exposure to secondhand smoke makes it more likely that kids will start smoking when they become teenagers. It also "makes it harder for adult smokers to quit."

AVOIDING PLAGIARISM WORKSHEET ANSWER KEY

Student Passage:

Everyone knows that smoking is bad for your health, and studies have shown that secondhand smoke isn't good for you either. About 50,000 Americans every year are killed by secondhand smoke, according to the Centers for Disease Control and Prevention (Miller 7). In addition, <u>a recent study has found that inhaling secondhand smoke affects the brain in much the same was as smoking a cigarette does</u>. {direct quote with no quotation marks or citation}. That means if you smoke around your child, the smoke may be affecting your child's brain as much as your own. <u>Exposure to secondhand smoke makes it more likely that kids will start smoking when they become teenagers.</u> {Paraphrased, but only slightly changed, and no citation} <u>It also "makes it harder for adult smokers to quit."</u> {no citation}

MLA FORMATTING

The basics for MLA formatting are covered here, but you may have a special source or formatting question that requires further information. The best comprehensive source for MLA information is the Online Writing Lab at Purdue University found here:

https://owl.english.purdue.edu/owl/resource/747/01/

Page Format

- Double space the whole paper, including the Works Cited page.

- Use an easily readable 12-point font, such as Times New Roman.

- The margins of the paper all the way around are 1 inch.

- Use the tab key (5 spaces) when beginning a new paragraph.

- Put your last name and page number in the upper right corner of each page, 1/2 inch from the top of the page.

- On the first page, in the upper left, one inch from the top of the page, list your name, the instructor's name, the class and the date. The date should be in this format: 21 March 2015.

- Center the title. Do not use a different, larger or bold font. Do not put extra space between the title and the text of the paper.

Here is a sample of the first page of an essay in MLA format:

Bailey Grayson

Torres

English 105

21 January 2016

Teaching an Old Dog New Tricks

Ever since I was a kid, I hated dogs. Everyone in my family was a cat person. My dad especially disliked the barking, annoying dogs in our neighborhood. Cats were clean, quiet, demanded little work, and did their business in a designated box filled with litter. Best of all, they didn't mind if you left them for a few days, as long as they had a supply of food and clean water.

Dogs, on the other hand, barked, slobbered, pooped wherever they wanted, and required daily walks. My best friend's dog, Linus, didn't help my impression of the canine species. He was a gigantic, bony thing who chased my friend as she tore around her deck on her Big Wheel. She laughed hysterically, but I cowered in the corner of the yard, certain she'd be eaten, or at best, pinned down and drooled on.

So when my family decided to get a rescue dog for my brother, not only was I surprised, but I vowed to have nothing to do with it. I put down the ground rules: I didn't want it in my room, I didn't want to see any poop on our front lawn, and it better never, ever slobber

IN-TEXT CITATIONS

When you quote or paraphrase a source in a paper, you **must** include an in-text citation. The citation comes directly after the quote or paraphrase. The punctuation for the sentence goes after the citation. Here are the general rules for in-text citations:

- If you have an author and page number: (last name of author pg #) = (Smith 32)

- If you mention the author's name in the same sentence as the quote or paraphrase, you do not need the author's name in the in-text citation: Smith stated that mortality rates for these infants are declining (32).

- If you have an author but no page number: (author) = (Smith)

- If you two authors: (author and author pg#) = (Smith, Herzog, and Chen, 32)

- If you have three or more authors: (author et al. pg #) = (Smith et al. 32)

- If you have multiple articles from the same author: (author, title pg #) = (Smith, "Critical Infant Care" 32)

- If you do not have an author: (title, page #) = ("Critical Infant Care" 32)

- If you do not have an author or title: (organization) = (American Nursing Association)

Following is a flow chart that will help you figure out your in-text citations.

IN-TEXT CITATION CHART

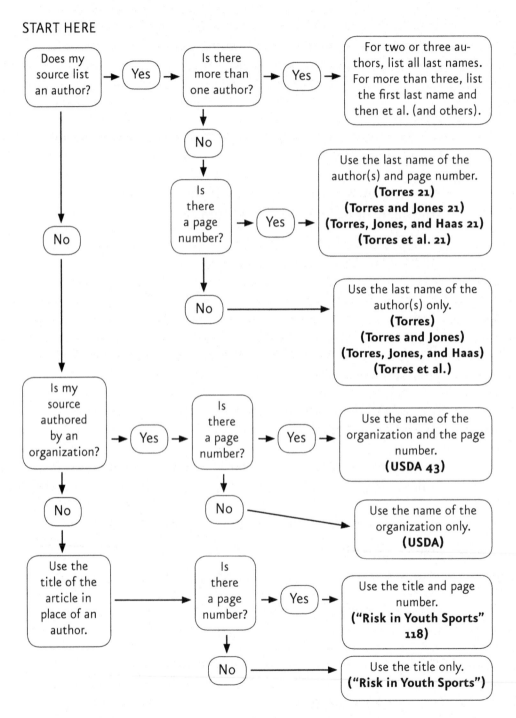

START HERE

Does my source list an author? → **Yes** → Is there more than one author? → **Yes** → For two or three authors, list all last names. For more than three, list the first last name and then et al. (and others).

Is there more than one author? → **No** → Is there a page number? → **Yes** → Use the last name of the author(s) and page number.
(Torres 21)
(Torres and Jones 21)
(Torres, Jones, and Haas 21)
(Torres et al. 21)

Is there a page number? → **No** → Use the last name of the author(s) only.
(Torres)
(Torres and Jones)
(Torres, Jones, and Haas)
(Torres et al.)

Does my source list an author? → **No** → Is my source authored by an organization? → **Yes** → Is there a page number? → **Yes** → Use the name of the organization and the page number.
(USDA 43)

Is there a page number? → **No** → Use the name of the organization only.
(USDA)

Is my source authored by an organization? → **No** → Use the title of the article in place of an author. → Is there a page number? → **Yes** → Use the title and page number.
("Risk in Youth Sports" 118)

Is there a page number? → **No** → Use the title only.
("Risk in Youth Sports")

WORKS CITED PAGE

The last page of your essay should be a Works Cited page. The page should be double-spaced with the title (Worked Cited) centered. Each entry should be alphabetized.

The Works Cited page contains core information about each source you used in your paper. No matter what kind of sources you used, look for the items in the following list. Not every source will have every item. After you have all the relevant information, create the listing in the same order as the list.

- Author
- Title of source
- Title of container
- Other contributors
- Version
- Number
- Publisher
- Publication date
- Location

Here is a detailed look at each item in the list.

Author

The author's name should be listed with the last name first: Wilson, Erin.

If there is more than one author, only the first author is listed last name first:

Wilson, Erin, and Aaron Wong.

If there are three or more authors, list the first author, last name first, and "et al." (et al. means "and others"):

Wilson, Erin, et al.

If there is no person who is listed as the author, this spot can be filled by an editor or translator. If the person listed is not the author, add a description as well. If there is more than one editor or translator, use the same rules as those for more than one author:

Giantonio, Richard, editor.

Giantonio, Richard, and Garrett Skraitz, editors.

Schneider, Steven, translator.

If a group (a corporation or foundation, for example) is responsible for the work, use the group's name in the author's place:

American Heart Association.

Centers for Disease Control.

For a movie or television show, use the director, screenwriter, performer, or whomever you are focusing on in your paper:

Spurlock, Morgan, director.

Title of source

The title of the work comes next. It will either be in italics or placed in quotation marks.

A larger, self-contained, independent work such as a book or collection of stories or poems, a movie, or a website uses italics:

Stegner, Wallace. *Crossing to Safety*.

Spurlock, Morgan, director. *Supersize Me*.

The title of a shorter work that is part of a collection, such as an essay, article, or poem, or part of a larger whole, such as an episode in a television series, is placed in quotation marks.

Eytan, Ted, et al. "Social Media and the Health System."

Title of container

MLA defines a larger format that contains your source as the "container." A container can be, for example, a book, journal, magazine, website, or television series. It can also be a database such as JSTOR or EBSCO, or a platform such as Netflix. The container is usually italicized, following the rule of titles:

Eytan, Ted, et al. "Social Media and the Health System." *The Permanente Journal,*

Sometimes a source can have more than one container. For example, an article's first container might be a journal, and the journal's container may be a database. In this case, you will want to find the relevant information for the second (and third, if applicable) container on the list from **Title of Container** to **Location**. The second container comes after information directly related to the first container:

Desonie, Dana. "Climate Change." *Atmosphere,* Chelsea House, 2007. *Science Online,*

Other contributors

If there are other contributors to the work that are important for the identification of the work, aside from the authors, name them and the description of their contribution:

Grass, Gunter. *Novemberland: Selected Poems,* 1956-1993. Translated by Michael Hamburger,

"The Heroin Epidemic." *60 Minutes,* reported by Bill Whitaker, produced by Tom Anderson,

Version

If your source has been released in more than one form, it might have a notation of version. This is commonly an edition or abridgement:

Langer, Susanne. "Language and Thought." Exploring Language, edited by Gary Goshgarian, 14th edition,

Number

A source may be part of a sequence, for example, a volume of a book set, or a journal volume and issue number. Use abbreviations to indicate volume (vol.) and number (no.):

Cózar, Andrés, et al. "Plastic Debris in the Open Ocean." *Proceedings of the National Academy of Sciences* vol. 111 no. 28

Publisher

The organization responsible for producing the source is the publisher. The publisher can be a traditional book or periodical publisher, a production studio for film and television shows, or an organization behind a website. You do not need to list a publisher for periodicals (newspapers, magazines, journals), if the name of the publisher is the same as the name of the website, or if the author or organization responsible for producing the work is the same:

Clark, C. *Mathematical Bioeconomics*. John Wiley and Sons Inc.,

Publication Date

Look for the day, month, and year of the publication date when available. Some sources will only have a month and year, some only the year. Sometimes a source will have multiple dates. For example, an online version of an article may have appeared in print at an earlier date, or a book may list the dates for several editions. In this case, use the date of the version you are using, and do not include the other dates.

Conniff, Richard. "Our Natural History, Endangered." *The New York Times*. 1 April 2016,

Clark, C. *Mathematical Bioeconomics*. John Wiley and Sons Inc., 1990.

Location

The location of a source can mean a page or page numbers. Use p. for page and pp. for pages:

Clark, C. *Mathematical Bioeconomics*. John Wiley and Sons Inc., 1990, pp. 86–88.

The location can also be a web address, URL, or DOI number:

Conniff, Richard. "Our Natural History, Endangered." *The New York Times*. 1 April 2016, http://www.nytimes.com/2016/04/03/opinion/ournatural-history-endangered.html

A web address can frequently change, so if there is a DOI (digital object identifier), include this instead of the webpage URL. The DOI will not change, even if the URL changes. Sometimes just the DOI number is listed, and sometimes the DOI will be imbedded in a link (this is different from the webpage link). Provide the link when given:

Bender, Kimberly, et al. "Interventions for Reducing Adolescent Alcohol Abuse." *Archives of Pediatrics and Adolescent Medicine*, vol. 164 no. 1, 2016, p. 85. http://dx.doi.org/10.1001/archpediatrics.2009.235

The location can also include information such as a disc number for a DVD set, the physical location of a piece of art or place where you attended a performance or lecture:

Pulsipher, Paige. "Etsy Entrepeneurs." Women in Business Forum. 21 March 2016, Folsom, CA.

Pollock, Jackson. One: Number 31: 1950. 1950, Museum of Modern Art, New York.

Optional Elements

There may be other items you wish to include in your entry. Any of these, or other relevant information, can be added to the end of the entry, or where they logically belong within the entry:

- Date of original publication
- Information about a prior publication
- City of publication
- Multiple volumes or name of series
- Description of unusual source
- Number and session of Congress when citing a government bill or report
- Date of access

The date of access can be important for online sources, which can be edited or changed.

The following charts give some example Works Cited entries and show a method for tracking your source information.

EXAMPLE 1

Author	.	Susanne Langer
Title of Source	.	Language and Thought
Title of Container	,	Exploring Language
Other Contributors	,	Gary Goshgarian
Version	,	14th edition
Number	,	
Publisher	,	Pearson
Publication Date	,	2015
Location	.	Pages 118-122

The Works Cited entry would look like this:

Langer, Susanne. "Language and Thought." *Exploring Language*, edited by Gary Goshgarian, 14th edition, Pearson, 2015, pp. 118–122.

EXAMPLE 2

Author	.	Dana Desonie
Title of Source	.	Climate Change
Title of Container	,	Atmosphere
Other Contributors	,	
Version	,	
Number	,	
Publisher	,	Chelsea House
Publication Date	,	2007
Location	.	

SECOND CONTAINER

Title of Container	,	Science Online
Other Contributors	,	
Version	,	
Number	,	
Publisher	,	
Publication Date	,	
Location	.	http://online.infobase.com/HRC/ Search/Details/371515?q= climatechange atmosphere

The Works Cited entry would look like this:

Desonie, Dana. "Climate Change." *Atmosphere*, Chelsea House, 2007. *Science Online*. http://online.infobase.com/HRC/Search/Details/371515?q=climatechange atmosphere.

EXAMPLE 3

Author	.	
Title of Source	.	The Heroine Epidemic
Title of Container	,	60 Minutes
Other Contributors	,	Bill Whitaker, reporter; Tom Anderson, producer
Version	,	
Number	,	
Publisher	,	
Publication Date	,	April 24th, 2016
Location	.	

SECOND CONTAINER

Title of Container	,	cbsnews.com
Other Contributors	,	
Version	,	
Number	,	
Publisher	,	
Publication Date	,	
Location	.	http://www.cbsnews.com/videos/the-heroin-epidemic-dialing-for-dollars-gold-star-parents/

The Works Cited entry would look like this:

"The Heroin Epidemic." *60 Minutes*, reported by Bill Whitaker, produced by Tom Anderson, cbsnews.com, 24 April 2016, http://www.cbsnews.com/videos/the-heroin-epidemic-dialing-for-dollars-gold-star-parents/.

Here is a blank chart to use for practice or to keep track of your own sources.

MLA CITATION CORE ELEMENTS WORKSHEET

Author	.	
Title of Source	.	
Title of Container	,	
Other Contributors	,	
Version	,	
Number	,	
Publisher	,	
Publication Date	,	
Location	.	

SECOND CONTAINER

Title of Container	,	
Other Contributors	,	
Version	,	
Number	,	
Publisher	,	
Publication Date	,	
Location	.	

CITATION PRACTICE WORKSHEET

Name: _____

For the following sources, create an in-text citation and a Works Cited entry. Assume that the information was taken from a web page.

● ● ●   Journal of American Medical Pro   +

← ⟳ | www.jamp.org/archives/articles/new-dietary-guidelines-on-total-fat.html   ▽ | → | Q | ↓ ⌂ ★ 🖺 ♡ 🔖 ◢ | ≡

JAMP.org
Journal of American Medical Professionals

Home | Current Issue | Archives | Subscribe

New Dietary Guidelines on Total Fat
John Prozarian, MD; Kenneth Lancing, PhD
July 5, 2013, Volume 95, No. 7, Pages 210-232

> New recommendations by the Dietary Advisory Committee indicate that dietary guidelines should be more discerning about fat. Rather than limiting all fats, Americans should be encouraged to consumer appropriate amounts of healthful fats.

In-text citation: (_____)

Works Cited entry: _____

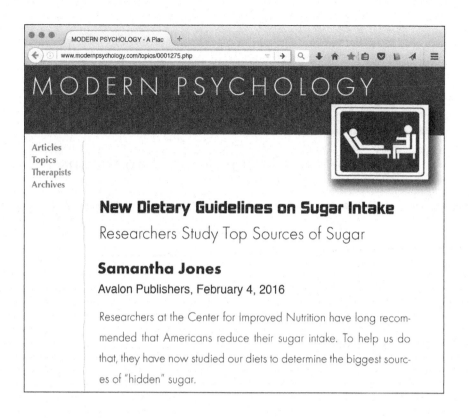

New Dietary Guidelines on Sugar Intake

Researchers Study Top Sources of Sugar

Samantha Jones

Avalon Publishers, February 4, 2016

Researchers at the Center for Improved Nutrition have long recommended that Americans reduce their sugar intake. To help us do that, they have now studied our diets to determine the biggest sources of "hidden" sugar.

In-text citation: (_____)

Works Cited entry: _____

In-text citation: (_____)

Works Cited entry: _____

CITATION PRACTICE WORKSHEET ANSWER KEY

1. In-text citation: (Prozarian and Lansing 210)

Works Cited entry: Prozarian, John, and Kenneth Lansing. "New Dietary Guidelines on Total Fat." *JAMP*, vol. 95, no. 7, 5 July 2013, 210–232. www.jamp.org/archives/articles/new-dietary-guidelines-on-total-fat.html.

2. In-text citation: (Jones)

Works Cited entry: Jones, Samantha. "New Dietary Guidelines on Sugar Intake." *Modern Psychology*, Avalon Publishers. 4 February 2016. www.modernpsychology.com/topics/0001275.php.

3. In-text citation: (USDON)

Works Cited entry: USDON. "Dietary Guidance for Americans." *USDON Center for Healthy Eating*, www.usdon.gov/archives/files/document=ID?49039763.

CHAPTER FOUR

SUMMARY/RESPONSE ESSAYS

Summary and response essays are a great way to practice critical reading, summarizing, and constructing arguments. This type of essay is also an introduction to the skills necessary for a research paper.

To decide on a topic, you can look at the ideas in the Writing Prompts section on pages 216–217, or choose your own idea.

You will need to choose one academic article for this assignment. See the guidelines on pages 72–73 to make sure you have chosen a qualifying article. Also, make sure it is substantial enough for you to write about, but not so large that it would be cumbersome to summarize. Look for an article with a focused topic that is not much longer than six pages in length.

On the following pages, you will find a sample academic article and a sample student essay in response to the article.

SAMPLE ARTICLE

Genetically Modified Foods: A Vicious Cycle

by Jamie McGuire

There are potential adverse health effects on consumers any time a new genetically modified (GM) product, or strain, is introduced into the food chain. In an article discussing GM organisms, John Pickrell points out, "genetic engineering allows exotic traits from unrelated species to be introduced." This genetic engineering also increases the potential for adverse effects on consumers. In addition, new adverse health effects on consumers of GM foods invites pharmaceutical companies to invent more drugs that can respond to those effects. Ironically, these drugs will likely be produced by the same corporations that introduced the new strains of food to us in the first place. This, then, gives those corporations, primarily the behemoth Monsanto, the opportunity to create, and profit from, this vicious cycle.

By producing these new strains of food, there is also the opportunity to introduce new toxins and/or allergens into the environment. Genetically modified foods introduce new proteins into the food chain, "from the organisms that are never part of food" (Grover 189). People who have allergies can be affected by these foreign proteins. GM soy that is consumed in the United States contains a gene that creates a protein that was never before part of the human food supply. Parts of that protein are the same as those found in shrimp and dust mite allergens. According to the World Health Organization's criteria, this fact should have prevented GM soy from being approved (Smith 2). A human feeding study showed that the gene put into soybeans was able to transfer out of food and into the DNA of gut bacteria. This means that the bacteria inside our intestines could potentially create the novel protein inside of us. If it is allergenic or toxic, there could be long-term effects from it, even if the soy was eliminated from the diet (Smith 2). The addition of new allergens and toxins into the environment and human diet creates the need for even more products to be introduced to counteract them.

Genetically modified foods also contain antibiotic-resistant genes. This also creates the potential to produce new "toxic proteins or transferring antibiotic-resistance and other genes to human gut bacteria to damaging effect" (Pickrell). Organizations all around the world, including the American Medical Association and the World Health Organization, are concerned about the ability of these genes to transfer out of food and into the DNA of gut bacteria just like in soybeans, which could create a whole new set of antibiotic-resistant "super" diseases (Smith 2). This, in turn, will contribute to another vicious cycle that we already live in, whereby we produce a resistance to antibiotics. This possibility once again invites corporations such as Monsanto to invent new drugs or antibiotics to respond to the resistance, further complicating the need and use for pharmaceuticals.

Proponents of GM foods argue that hearty strains of food that are, for example, pest-resistant and drought-resistant, will help solve world hunger issues. In theory, this sounds promising, but due to the exclusive patent held by Monsanto over one of the most crucial processes in agricultural biotechnology, there is no incentive for Monsanto to produce seeds for countries that cannot afford their product. Monsanto now sells beneficial seeds to farmers at monopolistic prices. While private sector research might benefit through the funding provided by Monsanto, application of these technologies in the parts of the world that need it most has been limited (Barrows, et al. 114).

While Monsanto has a dangerous monopoly over one of the most crucial processes in the use of agricultural biotechnology, they have the power to adversely affect the health of entire populations. Even though there may be potential benefits to GM organisms, we have not had enough time to determine whether or not the benefits outweigh the detrimental impacts on the environment, consumers, or the pharmaceutical world. As long as companies like Monsanto can keep exclusive rights over such potentially beneficial technologies, only they are in a position to truly benefit from the use of those technologies. The United States government should not allow exclusive patents that can have such wide-ranging detrimental effects on the global food supply. In addition, the production of GM foods should be banned until further studies can prove that GM foods are safe, and until no single corporation, or small group of corporations, can profit from the benefits and detriments of GM foods.

SAMPLE STUDENT SUMMARY/RESPONSE ESSAY

Kelly Carmen

Torres

English 155

21 March 2016

Summary and Response: Banning Genetically Modified Foods

In Jamie McGuire's article, "Genetically Modified Foods: A Vicious Cycle," she argues that genetically modified (GM) foods should be banned. McGuire's two main arguments for this ban are: first, that GM foods have potentially adverse effects on consumers' health and second, that companies such as Monsanto, which produce GM seeds, would also profit from producing medication to treat adverse effects, creating a "vicious cycle." McGuire believes that the United States should prohibit GM foods until they can be proven safe and until the Monsanto monopoly on the technology is broken.

While I agree that Monsanto has too much power over the industry and consumer choices, McGuire's proposal to ban all GM foods is too extreme. What McGuire leaves out of her article are the benefits that come from GM foods, the choices GM foods make available to consumers, and the lack of evidence showing that GM foods are truly dangerous.

There are undeniable benefits of GM foods. Some can with-stand more extreme conditions such as drought and cold weather than regular crops. There are also strains that are pest-resistant, re-quiring less use of dangerous and expensive pesticides. This could be a boon in areas of the world where crops are currently difficult to grow. Although McGuire points out that Monsanto sells these seeds at "monopolistic" (2) prices, she does mention that private sector research has benefitted from funding from Monsanto. She states, however, that the application of the technology in needy areas of the world has been "limited" (2). This does not mean that poor areas cannot benefit in the future. It would be a disservice to cut off this research that could potentially help to end world hunger issues. In addition, any crop that uses fewer resources and is more efficient to grow benefits everyone.

Banning GM foods would eliminate many foods that are reg-ularly purchased by consumers, including those containing corn and soy. According to the United States Department of Agriculture, in 2014, 88 percent of corn and 94 percent of soy grown in the United States was genetically modified (USDA). It would be virtually im-possible to eliminate all GM foods from American shelves. Instead of an outright ban, as McGuire suggests, it would be more logical to require labels on products made with GM foods so consumers can make the choice whether to purchase and consume them.

There is no definitive science on whether or not GM foods are dangerous or pose any health risk. In fact, a review of the published studies on GM foods between 2002 and 2012 showed that GM foods "appear to be safe" (Timmer). That does not mean there will not be studies in the future showing some problems, and the authors of the study said the results were "confusing at best" (Timmer), but banning GM foods based on nothing but speculation would do more harm than good.

McGuire makes a good point when she sounds the alarm that the technology and profits of GM foods are essentially in one company's hands, and this should certainly be addressed by the United States government, but GM foods have benefits that should be carefully considered before calling for an outright ban. The government should consider more moderate measures such as labeling and requiring Monsanto to share some exclusive patents for the good of all.

Works Cited

McGuire, Jamie. "Genetically Modified Foods: A Vicious Cycle." Heald College. 2015.

Timmer, John. "What Science Tells Us About the Safety of Genetically Modified Foods." *Scientific Method*, 4 October 2013. http://arstechnica.com/science/2013/10/what-science-tells-us-about-the-safety-of-genetically-modified-foods/.

USDA. "Adoption of Genetically Engineered Crops in the U.S." *usda.gov*. 14 July 2014. http://www.ers.usda.gov/data-products/adoption-of-genetically-engineered-crops-in-the-us.aspx.

SUMMARY/RESPONSE ESSAY ASSIGNMENT

Write a 1 1/2 to 2 page typed, double-spaced summary/response essay.

- Choose one article that qualifies as an academic source.

- Carefully read the article and summarize the thesis and main points in an objective manner, attributing all ideas and opinions to the author. This will become the first paragraph of your essay.

- In the next paragraph, respond to the article with a thesis statement, where you agree or disagree with points in the article.

- Write body paragraphs and a conclusion based on your thesis, referring back to the article frequently.

The grading criteria is as follows:

Summary: 25 points
> The summary is clear, objective, and covers only the main points of the article. The ideas are attributed to the article's author.

Thesis: 15 points
> The thesis is clear and is an appropriate and reasoned response to the article.

Body Paragraphs: 15 points
> Each body paragraph contains clear topic sentences that support the thesis and introduce a main idea that will be

covered in the paragraph. Paragraphs are well organized.

Use of Article: 15 points

The article is referred to effectively in the body of the essay.

Logic and Evidence: 10 points

Personal knowledge, experience, and/or outside evidence supports logical arguments.

Conclusion: 10 points

The conclusion revisits the main point of the article and is consistent with the response thesis.

Conventions: 10 points

The essay contains few grammatical and punctuation errors. Essay is in MLA format.

Total: 100 points

ANNOTATING AN ARTICLE

The first step in writing a summary and response essay is to thoroughly and critically read the article you will be addressing. When you read an article critically, you are not just seeking to understand what the author is saying, but questioning the author's points and analyzing why and how the ideas are presented. It is also important to consider how effectively the author presents the arguments.

Annotating the article will help you with this process. Annotating is basically a note-taking system directly on the article. Read through the article once, then get a highlighter and pencil and follow these steps as you re-read the article:

1. Read the article's title and first paragraph. Make a note in the margin about what expectations you might have for the article based on the introductory information. What is the author's topic? What is the tone? What might be the author's main point?

2. Locate and highlight the thesis of the article. If there is no single sentence that contains the thesis statement (an implied thesis), mark the sections where the author's main point is most evident. In the margin, write a "T" or an asterisk so you can quickly come back to the thesis.

3. Highlight any words that you don't know, or sections that you don't understand. Write a "?" in the margin so you can look up definitions later.

4. Highlight the main points in the article. These are often topic sentences. Write "MP" in the margin.

5. Make notes in the margin of any questions you might have. Why did the author use a certain example? What has the author left out?

6. Note any sections where the author has made an effective or ineffective point.

Genetically Modified Foods: A Vicious Cycle

by Jamie McGuire

author opposed to GM foods

what are the effects?

There are potential adverse health effects on consumers any time a new genetically modified (GM) product, or strain, is introduced into the food chain. In an article discussing GM organisms, John Pickrell points out, "genetic engineering allows exotic traits from unrelated species to be introduced." This genetic engineering also increases the potential for adverse effects on consumers. In addition, new adverse health effects on consumers of GM foods invites pharmaceutical companies to invent more drugs that can respond to those effects. Ironically, these drugs will likely be produced by the same corporations that introduced the new strains of food to us in the first place. This, then, gives those corporations, primarily the behemoth Monsanto, the opportunity to create, and profit from, this vicious cycle.

health effects main concern-MP

distrust of Monsanto

T

By producing these new strains of food, there is also the opportunity to introduce new toxins and/or allergens into the environment. Genetically modified foods introduce new proteins into the food chain, "from the organisms that are never part of food" (Grover 189). People who have allergies can be affected by these foreign proteins. GM soy that is consumed in the United States contains a gene that creates a protein that was never before part of the human

examples of health effects

food supply. Parts of that protein are the same as those found in shrimp and dust mite allergens. According to the World Health Organization's criteria, this fact should have prevented GM soy from being approved (Smith 2). A human feeding study showed that the [?] gene put into soybeans was able to transfer out of food and into the DNA of gut bacteria. This means that the bacteria inside our intes- [?] tines could potentially create the novel protein inside of us. If it is allergenic or toxic, there could be long-term effects from it, even if the soy was eliminated from the diet (Smith 2). The addition of new allergens and toxins into the environment and human diet creates the need for even more products to be introduced to counteract them.

examples of health effects

Genetically modified foods also contain antibiotic-resistant genes. This also creates the potential to produce new "toxic proteins or transferring antibiotic-resistance and other genes to human gut bacteria to damaging effect" (Pickrell). Organizations all around the world, including the American Medical Association and the World Health Organization, are concerned about the ability of these genes to transfer out of food and into the DNA of gut bacteria just like in soybeans, which could create a whole new set of antibiotic-resistant "super" diseases (Smith 2). This, in turn, will contribute to another vicious cycle that we already live in, whereby we produce a resistance to antibiotics. This possibility once again invites corporations such as Monsanto to invent new drugs or antibiotics to respond to the resistance, further complicating the need and use for pharmaceuticals.

specula-tion-in-effective. why only Monsanto?

Proponents of GM foods argue that hearty strains of food that are, for example, pest-resistant and drought-resistant will help solve world hunger issues. In theory, this sounds promising, but due to the exclusive patent held by Monsanto over one of the most crucial processes in agricultural biotechnology, there is no incentive for Monsanto to produce seeds for countries that cannot afford their product. Monsanto now sells beneficial seeds to farmers at monopolistic prices. While private sector research might benefit through the funding provided by Monsanto, application of these technologies in the parts of the world that need it most has been limited (Barrows, et al. 114).

effective point

couldn't it expand in the fu-ture? why cut off beneficial technolo-gy?

While Monsanto has a dangerous monopoly over one of the most crucial processes in the use of agricultural biotechnology, they have the power to adversely affect the health of entire populations. Even though there may be potential benefits to GM organisms, we have not had enough time to determine whether or not the benefits outweigh the detrimental impacts on the environment, consumers, or the pharmaceutical world. As long as companies like Monsanto can keep exclusive rights over such potentially beneficial technologies, only they are in a position to truly benefit from the use of those technologies. The United States government should not allow ex-

what are ben-efits?

clusive patents that can have such wide-ranging detrimental effects on the global food supply. In addition, the production of GM foods should be banned until further studies can prove that GM foods are safe, and until no single corporation, or small group of corporations, can profit from the benefits and detriments of GM foods. [T]

SUMMARIZING AN ARTICLE

After you have annotated your article, it's time to write a summary. Writing a summary gives your reader an objective, condensed version of the article. Most articles can be summarized in a few sentences or one short paragraph. If your summary goes longer than this, make sure you are not using details and examples from the article and are summarizing the main points only. You can address statistics, examples, and illustrations in the response section of the essay.

TIPS

- Give the reader context. Name the article and author in the first sentence.

- Keep it objective. Give the author's opinion only (no "I" statements, opinions, or analysis).

- Give the thesis and main points only. Do not use examples and illustrations.

- Attribute all ideas to the author. Use tags such as: According to the author . . . ; The author states . . . ; The author also believes . . .

- Use your own words (paraphrase). Avoid direct quotes. For emphasis, you may want to include a word or two from the original passage. In this case, be sure to use quotation marks.

SAMPLE STUDENT SUMMARY

Author
and name
of article
in first
sentence

main
point

In Jamie McGuire's article, "Genetically Modified Foods: A
Vicious Cycle," she argues that genetically modified (GM) foods
should be banned. McGuire's two main arguments for this ban are:
first, that GM foods have potentially adverse effects on consumers'
health and second, that companies such as Monsanto, which produce GM seeds, would also profit from producing medication to
treat adverse effects, creating a "vicious cycle." McGuire believes
that the United States should prohibit GM foods until they can be
proven safe and until the Monsanto monopoly on the technology is
broken.

main
point

author's
words in
quotations

author's
conclusion

To help you organize your thoughts before you start writing your
summary, go back to your annotated article and then use the Summary Graphic Organizer to outline the summary.

SUMMARY GRAPHIC ORGANIZER

Name _____

> ### Name of the article and author

> ### Author's thesis/opinion

> ### Main point

> ### Main point

> ### Main point

> ### Author's conclusion

WRITING A RESPONSE

Once you have an objective summary, it's time for your own opinion. Think about whether you agree or disagree with the author. It's common to agree with some points and disagree with others, so you will want to decide which points you want to address. You do not have to take on the entire article.

The first step is forming a working thesis, where you agree or disagree with the article, or points in the article. It's best to then list a few reasons why so you can set up the organization of the rest of your response. Here is the thesis statement from the sample summary and response essay:

> While I agree that the Monsanto company has too much power over the industry and consumer choices, McGuire's proposal to ban all GM foods is too extreme. What McGuire leaves out of her article are the benefits that come from GM foods, consumer choice, and the lack of evidence showing the GM foods are truly dangerous.

The first sentence clearly gives the author's response to the article. The second sentence then gives three reasons why the author disagrees with the article's main proposal. The three reasons will become topic sentences for three body paragraphs. The paper now has an outline:

Paragraph 1: Summary
Paragraph 2: Response thesis
Paragraph 3: Benefits of GM foods
Paragraph 4: Consumer choice
Paragraph 5: Lack of evidence that GM foods are dangerous
Paragraph 6: Conclusion

TIPS

- You can respond with your own experience and knowledge, but your response will be even more effective if you bring in evidence from outside sources to support your points.
- Be sure to give evidence and a logical argument whether you agree or disagree with a point.
- Stay close to the points in the article. It's easy to veer off on your own tangent about the topic, but remember that you are responding to what is in the article. Use quotes and paraphrase from the article throughout the response.
- Write a conclusion that is consistent with your thesis and comes back to the main point of the article.

SAMPLE STUDENT RESPONSE

Response thesis

topic sentence

Reasons that support thesis

While I agree that Monsanto has too much power over the industry and consumer choices, McGuire's proposal to ban all GM foods is too extreme. What McGuire leaves out of her article are the benefits that come from GM foods, the choices GM foods make available to consumers, and the lack of evidence showing that GM foods are truly dangerous.

There are undeniable benefits of GM foods. Some can withstand more extreme conditions such as drought and cold weather than regular crops. There are also strains that are pest-resistant, requiring less use of dangerous and expensive pesticides. This could be a boon in areas of the world where crops are currently difficult to grow. Although McGuire points out that Monsanto sells these seeds at "monopolistic" (2) prices, she does mention that private sector research has benefitted from funding from Monsanto. She states, however, that the application of the technology in needy areas of the world has been "limited" (2). This does not mean that poor areas cannot benefit in the future. It would be a disservice to cut off this research that could potentially help to end world hunger issues. In addition, any crop that uses fewer resources and is more efficient to grow benefits everyone.

reference to article

Banning GM foods would eliminate many foods that are regularly purchased by consumers, including those containing corn and soy. According to the United States Department of Agriculture, in 2014, 88 percent of corn and 94 percent of soy grown in the United States was genetically modified (USDA). It would be virtually impossible to eliminate all GM foods from American shelves. Instead of an outright ban, as McGuire suggests, it would be more logical to require labels on products made with GM foods so consumers can make the choice whether to purchase and consume them.

topic sentence

evidence supp poi

reference to article

There is no definitive science on whether or not GM foods are dangerous or pose any health risk. In fact, a review of the published studies on GM foods between 2002 and 2012 showed that GM foods "appear to be safe" (Timmer). That does not mean there will not be studies in the future showing some problems, and the authors of the study said the results were "confusing at best" (Timmer), but

topic sentence

evidence supp poi

banning GM foods based on nothing but speculation would do more harm than good.

Refer back to main point of article in conclusion

McGuire makes a good point when she sounds the alarm that the technology and profits of GM foods are essentially in one company's hands, and this should certainly be addressed by the United States government, but GM foods have benefits that should be carefully considered before calling for an outright ban. The government should consider more moderate measures such as labeling and requiring Monsanto to share some exclusive patents for the good of all.

Conclusion consistent with thesis

ROUGH DRAFT

Now it's time to write a rough draft. This draft is meant to be a starting place, so don't worry about getting everything perfect. You will have plenty of time to revise and make improvements later.

After you have your rough draft, do the following steps to revise:

1. Get at least two people to read your rough draft and critique it, using the Summary/Response Essay Critique worksheet.

2. Complete the Next Step worksheet.

After completing these steps, it is helpful to write another draft, revise, proofread, and then write your final draft.

SUMMARY/RESPONSE ESSAY CRITIQUE

Your Name: _____

Author's Name: _____

Write your comments directly on the draft. These questions will help direct your critique.

SUMMARY (FIRST PARAGRAPH)

1. Does the writer introduce the name of the article and the author in the first sentence?

2. Is the summary completely objective? Mark any places where you find the writer's opinion or analysis.

3. Does the summary contain only the thesis and main points? Mark any unnecessary details or examples.

4. Are all the ideas and opinions attributed to the author? Mark any places that need attribution.

RESPONSE

1. Is the thesis statement clear? Does it agree or disagree with a point or points in the article?

2. Does each body paragraph have a topic sentence? Is each paragraph logical and does it offer support for the topic?

3. Do the body paragraphs refer back to the article?

4. Does the conclusion refer back to the main point of the article? Is it consistent with the response thesis?

NEXT STEP WORKSHEET

Name: _____

What are three things I learned about my essay from my critiques?

    1. _____

    2. _____

    3. _____

What two things do I need to do next to improve my essay? (List more if desired.)

    1. _____

    2. _____

SUMMARY/RESPONSE GRADING RUBRIC

Summary /25 points

The summary is clear, objective, and covers only the main points of the article. The ideas are attributed to the article's author.

Thesis /15 points

The thesis is clear and is an appropriate and reasoned response to the article.

Body Paragraphs /15 points

Each body paragraph contains a clear topic sentence that supports the thesis and introduces a main idea that will be covered in the paragraph. Paragraphs are well organized.

Use of Article /15 points

The article is referred to effectively in the body of the essay.

Logic and Evidence /10 points

Personal knowledge, experience, and/or outside evidence support logical arguments.

Conclusion /10 points

The conclusion revisits the main point of the article and is consistent with the response thesis.

Conventions /10 points

The essay contains few grammatical and
punctuation errors. Essay is in MLA format.

_____

100 points total

Comments:

CHAPTER FIVE

RESEARCH PAPERS

A research paper is often confused with an informational essay. An informational essay tells the reader all about a topic. A research paper contains an argument about a topic. There is a big difference, because a research paper showcases your critical thinking skills in a way that an informational essay does not. For the research paper, you will be reviewing multiple sources, reaching a conclusion, and forming an opinion about a topic before you even begin writing. Your essay will then use the research to prove your point.

To help you choose a topic, you can look at the prompts on pages 216–217, or come up with your own idea.

SAMPLE STUDENT RESEARCH PAPER

Paulsen 1

Joel Paulsen

Torres

English 155

26 July 2016

Bariatric Surgery Reexamined: The Times Are Changing

In the 1970's and early 1980's, many people, both inside and outside the medical community, viewed bariatric surgical procedures as being radical, unnecessary, and dangerous. Early on, procedures such as Roux-en-Y gastric bypass (RYGB) and adjustable gastric banding (AGB) frequently resulted in complications ranging from infection, liver disease, and internal bleeding. As a result, the public at large came to the perception that these treatments were not safe. In the past 10 years, however, that opinion is being re-examined in light of some new and compelling evidence regarding the health and psychosocial benefits of bariatric surgery for adults as well as adolescents.

In the 2007 International Journal of Obesity article entitled "Long-Term Health and Psychosocial Outcomes from Surgically Induced Weight Loss," author Dr. EMH Mathus-Vliegen, related the findings of his team's study. They found that the benefits for morbidly obese patients (patients who have a Body Mass Index of 40 or greater) who elected to undergo gastric bypass surgery were more than just cosmetic. The author stated that his study found that there are long-term health benefits which positively impact the quality of life. In the article, Dr. Mathus-Vliegen concluded by suggesting that these long-term benefits are present even in cases in which the patient does not engage in a medically supervised post-surgical treatment plan.

While not being a requirement, a holistic post-treatment plan greatly improves the likelihood of long-term success. As an example, Dr. Mathus-Vliegen's study revealed that eight years after the operation, levels of anxiety, depression, positive well-being, and self-control in females had all returned to pre-operational levels (Mathus-Vliegen 301). In short, the study concluded that an "improving mental health and quality of life by the first year eroded over subsequent years" (Mathus-Vliegen 306). This speaks directly to the need for bariatric surgery patients to undergo an extensive post-surgical treatment plan that addresses the mental, emotional and psychological issues which, in many cases, contributed to the problem to begin with.

Today, nearly 20% of young people between 12 and 19 years of age are classified as being obese (Austin 254). There has never been a more comprehensive understanding of the negative long-term health risks associated with obesity in young people. This has led many people to the sober realization that for young and old alike, being severely overweight presents a more immediate health risk than almost any other single factor. While some would argue that the more traditional approaches, such as lifestyle changes, medication, and behavior modification, are adequate to address the issue, the fact is they have all proven largely ineffective. In addition, positive outcomes attributed to bariatric surgery have proven to be more immediate, pervasive, and lasting than previously thought. While it is true that the surgery has potential risks, the rewards far outweigh the potential complications. Bariatric surgery is a good option for obese children to safely lose weight.

The serious long-term health consequences related to being obese are known to all but the most uninformed. The myriad of diseases which have been linked with being obese include, but are not limited to, sleep apnea, hypertension, high cholesterol, and Type II diabetes (Austin 254). In recent years, rates of Type II diabetes have soared among children. If left untreated, it can lead to long-term organ damage resulting in death. Cardiovascular disease, which is the leading cause of death in the United States, is also closely linked to obesity. Treating diseases like cardiovascular disease early dramatically improves heart function in the long term. In fact, there is recent data which suggests that bariatric surgery can help reverse obesity-related ventricular enlargement in adolescents (Jenkins 3). Surgical treatment has long been accepted as an appropriate option for adults with chronic health conditions related to obesity, but until recently such procedures were considered inappropriate for treating adolescents with the same conditions. Ironically, data now suggests that bariatric surgery may actually be more effective for treating adolescents than adults. This is due to the fact that early surgical intervention prevents the development of many of the associated conditions related to long-term severe obesity.

Traditional approaches to weight loss, while useful for the

mild to moderately obese person, are ineffective for those who are extremely obese. It is common knowledge that lifestyle interventions, including behavior modification, physical activity education, goal setting, and family support take a substantial amount of time before yielding the desired results. Even if they are able to lose the initial weight, many find it is very difficult to maintain their weight loss for the long term. In the end, losing this battle results in lower self-esteem and even lower self-image. Treating morbid obesity with prescription drugs has also proven to be a far from ideal solution. While they are less invasive than surgery, many drugs have adverse side effects which cause pain, nausea, and, in some cases, more serious discomfort. Other weight loss drugs have been recalled completely by the United States Food and Drug Administration (FDA) due to concerns that their long-term use contributes to heart disease and other complications.

Recent data suggests that the positive outcomes of bariatric surgery are more immediate, pervasive, and lasting than previously thought. For example, one study showed that 10 out of 11 adolescents who underwent RYGB surgery were able to discontinue oral diabetic medication within one year (Jenkins 2). In addition, patients have seen improvement in weight loss due to their body's ability to burn fat after undergoing bariatric surgery. This change is more lasting because it occurs at the physiological level.

For children there is even more good news. There is also substantial evidence that indicates that, in addition to weight loss, adolescents experience a reduction in instances of death from obesity-related conditions in adulthood. Adolescents who had bariatric surgery saw reduced cholesterol, triglycerides, and LDL levels. The evidence suggests that early surgical intervention in adolescents can actually help reverse some of the effects of cardiovascular disease. In addition to the physical health benefits, there are psychological benefits as well. Adolescents who elected to have surgery saw reduced instances of depression and increased perception of their self-image. However, according to Mathus-Vliegen, "some of these immediate psychological improvements can erode if not supported with effective follow up treatment plan" (305).

Bariatric surgery is an effective treatment for weight loss, but it is not without its risks and complications. Much of the perceived risk for adolescents and adults relates to the surgical procedure itself. In recent years, new techniques have been developed which have reduced the risk significantly. The risk from death is extremely low, especially when compared with the known risk of death related to extreme obesity. Probably the most consistent complications encountered as a result of bariatric surgery are nutritional deficiencies, resulting from the body's inability to absorb minerals and proteins. Vitamin D, Iron, Calcium, Vitamin B12, Zinc, and Vitamin C are all potentially negatively impacted by bariatric surgery. These deficiencies are caused by the diversion or removal of part of the stomach lining as a part of the bariatric surgical procedure. It is important that all patients who have bariatric surgery receive adequate supplementation to avoid issues with vitamin deficiency and bone-loss (Jenkins 6).

Adolescents who are suffering from being extremely obese are fortunate to live in this day and age where new options such as bariatric surgery exist and are available to help them. Bariatric surgery can be used as part of a holistic approach to reverse serious health conditions related to obesity. As a result of these procedures, adolescents are healthier, happier, and more confident.

At the same time, the role of personal responsibility and decision making for our health should not be eliminated. The way in which gastric bypass surgery and other weight loss surgical procedures are being marketed in our society as an "easy" solution all but guarantees that their use will continue to increase. Although there has been some slight improvement, our society still under-emphasizes the role that education, discipline, and moderation play in maintaining a healthy weight. The concern is that desperate people will engage in such drastic procedures without addressing the underlying causes, which will only lead to long-term pain and failure. Gastric bypass surgery, when used in conjunction with a comprehensive and holistic treatment plan, is a useful tool in the war against obesity, but it has its limitations and is by no means the miracle cure that some might believe.

Works Cited

Austin, Heather. "Bariatric Surgery in Adolescents: What's the rationale? What's rational?" *International Review of Psychiatry*, vol. 24, no. 3, June 2012, pp. 254–61, doi: 10.3109/09540261.2012.678815.

Jenkins, T. "Bariatric Surgery for Adolescents." *Pediatric Diabetes*, vol. 14, no. 1, February 2013, pp. 1–12, doi: 10.1111/j.1399-5448.2012.00899.x.

Mathus-Vliegen, E. M. "Long-term Health and Psychosocial Outcomes from Surgically Induced Weight Loss." *International Journal of Obesity*, vol. 31, no. 2, February 2007, pp. 299–307, http://www.ncbi.nlm.nih.gov/pubmed/16755282.

RESEARCH PAPER ASSIGNMENT

Write a research paper, 4–5 pages in length (not including Works Cited page), using at least three academic sources. Cite all sources and use MLA format.

The grading criteria is as follows:

Introduction: 10 points

The essay grabs the reader's attention, is interesting, and is relevant.

Thesis statement: 15 points

The thesis is clear, has an opinion, and fits the scope of the paper.

Organization: 15 points

The essay is logically organized. Paragraphs have topic sentences and clear transitions.

Research: 25 points

Outside sources are appropriate and effectively integrated into the essay. There is a proper balance of research and author opinion.

Conclusion: 10 points

The conclusion is effective, not just a re-statement of the thesis.

Conventions: 15 points

There are few errors in sentence structure, grammar, spelling and punctuation.

Citations: 10 points

> All outside sources are cited and the citations are in the correct format. The works cited page is included and in the proper format.

Total: 100 points

RESEARCH PAPER TIMELINE

Prewriting   Date Due: _____

Research/Article Worksheets   Date Due: _____

Working Thesis   Date Due: _____

Outline/Research Sandwiches Date Due: _____

Rough Draft (3 copies)   Date Due: _____

Final Draft   Date Due: _____

PREWRITING TECHNIQUES

Prewriting techniques are meant to help you get warmed up and start a free flow of ideas. This should be a low-stakes exercise where you don't have to worry about getting it "wrong."

To begin, try the prewriting techniques introduced on pages 22–30: the Brainstorming List, Clustering, and Free Writes.

Since a research paper will include an argument, also do the Arguments Worksheet.

BRAINSTORMING LIST

Name: _____

1. _____

2. _____

3. _____

4. _____

5. _____

6. _____

7. _____

8. _____

9. _____

10. _____

CLUSTERING

Set a timer for two minutes and make clusters of related ideas.

Name: _____

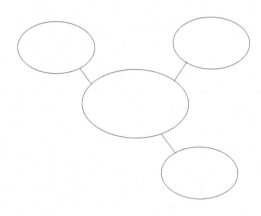

FREE WRITE

Name: _____

Set a timer for three minutes to write as much as you can on the ideas you circled on one of your clusters.

ARGUMENTS

Now that you have two or three good topics, use the Argument Worksheet to explore whether your topic can be an argument. If not, it is just informational, which is not what you want for this type of essay.

Here is an example of a student prewriting cluster.

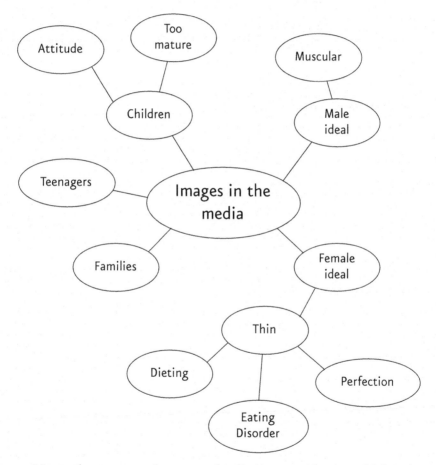

Using the topic in the example cluster, a student could develop an argument for an essay like this:

Topic: **Media and eating disorders.**

Argument: Media images can be a cause for eating disorders in girls.

Opposition: Eating disorders are caused by a mental illness and not the media.

This exercise will not only help you think through whether your topics have an argument, but also give a possible direction for your paper. Of course, your ideas will change as you start researching and delving into your topics, but it's helpful to have a possible direction in mind when you begin researching.

ARGUMENTS WORKSHEET

Name: _____

Topic: _____

Your Argument: _____

Possible Opposition: _____

Topic: _____

Your Argument: _____

Possible Opposition: _____

CONDUCTING RESEARCH

For a research paper, you will want to read as much on your topic as you can, and then select a few good sources to use in your paper. It is important that your sources are qualified academic sources. Review the material on pages 72–73 to make sure you are using appropriate sources.

It is helpful to take notes on your sources, or print them out and annotate them (see pages 106–107 for a review on annotating). You can also use the Source Worksheet to record your notes and keep track of the publication information for citations.

SOURCE WORKSHEET

Name: _____

Authors: _____

Title: _____

Source (website, journal, magazine, book): _____

Volume/Issue: _____

Publisher: _____

Page numbers: _____

Medium (web, print, DVD, personal interview): _____

Date of access (if online): _____

Summary of source: _____

_____

_____

_____

Notes and quotes: _____

_____

_____

_____

_____

_____

_____

_____

_____

_____

_____

THESIS STATEMENTS

What is a thesis statement?

A thesis statement is a guide to your paper. It tells the reader the subject matter, your argument, and what to expect from the rest of the paper. Usually, the thesis statement will come somewhere in the first paragraph.

Think of your first thesis as a "working thesis," or a statement that is likely to change. Often, once you get into the body of the paper, you may discover that your thesis needs to be changed a bit as you discover more information.

TIPS

- Make sure your thesis fits the scope of the paper. The scope means how long and how in-depth the research should be. If you only have two pages, you need to keep the thesis narrow enough to cover the argument adequately.

- Don't simply give a fact or make a statement that is obvious. For example, "An eating disorder is a serious disease" is a statement most would readily agree with. This is sometimes called a "so what?" thesis.

- You don't need to start your thesis with "I believe..." or "In my opinion..." You are the author of the paper, so this is obvious to the reader. Using these types of phrases weakens the power of your statement.

What is a good thesis statement?

Below are five thesis statements. The first four are problematic.

1. I'm going to discuss why people get eating disorders.

This statement is an announcement, not a thesis. There is no opinion or argument. It's very broad, and it seems the paper will be informational. Also, it's not very catchy; how many people will want to read on?

2. There are many reasons someone might develop an eating disorder.

This is a "so what?" thesis. Your reader likely already knows this. There is nothing new or compelling. It's broad, and it lacks an argument.

3. Some people might think the media contributes to eating disorders.

This is better, but who are "some people" and why do we care what they "might" think? This statement is starting to develop an argument, but since it is attributed to "some people," it lacks any punch.

4. Media images are the reason girls develop eating disorders.

This is clear and definitely has an argument. So what's wrong? It's a statement that can't be supported by the research. You'd be hard pressed to find any academic source that would make the claim that images in the media are the only reason girls develop eating disorders.

5. Although researchers believe that the cause for eating disorders is complicated, media images are one of the main reasons girls develop these disorders.

This thesis statement shows that you've done your research, and have come to a reasonable argument about the cause of eating disorders. The reader knows what to expect from the rest of the essay—that you will show why you think this is so, even though there is opposition to the argument.

WRITE A WORKING THESIS

On the Thesis Worksheet, try writing a working thesis for your paper based on the prewriting and preliminary research you have done, then answer the questions underneath. If you can't answer yes to any of the questions, try again. Remember, you can always come back and change your working thesis, so don't worry if it's not perfect at this point.

THESIS WORKSHEET

Name: _____

Topic: _____

Argument:_____

Working Thesis: _____

Is my thesis clear? _____

Does my thesis fit the scope of the paper? _____

Does my thesis contain an argument? _____

Can I support the argument with research? _____

Does the reader know what to expect from the rest of the paper?_____

THESIS WORKSHEET

Topic:_____

Argument: _____

Working Thesis: _____

Is my thesis clear? _____

Does my thesis fit the scope of the paper? _____

Does my thesis contain an argument? _____

Can I support the argument with research? _____

Does the reader know what to expect from the rest of the paper? _____

OUTLINE

Once you have your working thesis statement and your sources, it's time to organize your essay with an outline. Fill in each blank with a short note so you stay on track as you write.

Working Thesis:

Topic: _____

Supporting detail: _____

Supporting detail: _____

Supporting detail: _____

Topic: _____

Supporting detail: _____

Supporting detail: _____

Supporting detail: _____

Topic: _____

Supporting detail: _____

Supporting detail: _____

Supporting detail: _____

BODY PARAGRAPHS

You've got your topic, you've got your research, and you've got a working thesis. Now how do you put it all together? If you learn the basic building block of the body paragraph—the research sandwich—your job will be a lot easier. Your introduction and conclusion will probably be structured a little differently, and not every paragraph will follow this format, but it's a good place to start. This method also helps you to achieve the right balance of your own words and of research in the paper, which should be about half and half.

THE "RESEARCH SANDWICH"

As a general rule, each body paragraph will comprise one or more building blocks we'll call "research sandwiches." This is the formula:

Your own words (topic sentence with your opinion)

Research (direct quote or paraphrase to back up your opinion)

Your own words (analysis, summary or transition to the next topic)

Let's say your paper is about how you believe that media images of ultra-thin models contribute to eating disorders in females. This is what a body paragraph might look like, using the research sandwich method:

	If young girls are constantly exposed to pictures of beautiful, thin women, they might think that they must conform to this ideal to be considered attractive and become unhappy with their bodies. **One study found that exposure to media images decreases body satisfaction in girls (Wertheim et al, 47). Researcher James Thomas states that this body dissatisfaction occurs when "the individual accepts societal views of ideal weight and attractiveness and acts in a certain way to achieve the ideal body"(93).** When girls are not happy with the way they look, they may turn to crash diets or other unhealthy eating habits in order to try and conform to an unrealistic standard of beauty.

Your words — If young girls...

Research — One study...

Your words — When girls...

A research sandwich can stand alone as a paragraph, or you can put two or three together, if the ideas are closely related, to form one longer paragraph.

It's important to include smooth transitions from one "sandwich" to the next. Sometimes this can be accomplished in the concluding sentence of the sandwich, or in the next topic sentence, but be sure you think about the transition so your paper doesn't seem to jump from topic to topic.

Here's an example of a smooth transition from one sandwich to the next:

	If young girls are constantly exposed to pictures of beautiful, thin women, they might think that they must conform to this ideal to be considered attractive and become unhappy with their bodies. **One study found that exposure to media images decreases body satisfaction in girls (Wertheim et al., 47). Research-**
Your words	
Research	

Your words — If young girls are constantly exposed to pictures of beautiful, thin women, they might think that they must conform to this ideal to be considered attractive and become unhappy with their bodies. **One study found that exposure to media images decreases body satisfaction in girls (Wertheim et al., 47). Research-**

Research — **er James Thomas states that this body dissatisfaction occurs when "the individual accepts societal views of ideal weight and attractiveness and acts in a certain way to achieve the ideal body"(93).** When girls are not happy with the way they look, they may turn to crash diets or other unhealthy eating habits in or-

Your words — der to try and conform to an unrealistic standard of beauty. Since the ideal is not based in reality, dieting

Transition — often leads to perceived failure, causing even more extreme eating habits. This combination of ongoing

Your words — unhappiness with their bodies and unhealthy dieting is one of the greatest risk factors that leads girls to eating disorders. **Kathryn Miller states that these two factors together "are responsible for adolescent females being particularly vulnerable to eating disorders" (441). Miller also points out that these risk**

Research — **factors can begin many years before the actual eating disorder emerges (441).** Young girls, then, who are exposed to media images may start to develop risk

Your words — factors even before they are out of elementary school.

This section could be one paragraph, or broken into two paragraphs, but either way, you still need a smooth transition between ideas.

Sometimes it is helpful to work on research sandwiches individually, decide how to order them in the paper, and then work on transitions. Many students, though, find it helpful to outline the order of the ideas before working on the sandwiches. Whichever way you choose to draft your essay, you will find the following worksheets helpful in organizing and writing your ideas. You may need to go back to your outline and adjust the number of topics or details after you have finished the research sandwich worksheets.

Start by writing your working thesis in the space on Worksheet #1 (Remember, your thesis might change as you work on the body of the paper.) Fill in the rest of the worksheet, then move to Worksheet #2 and so on. Write an idea for a transition on the top of the worksheets. This will help you keep your ideas organized.

SANDWICH WORKSHEET—TOPIC 1  RESEARCH

Working Thesis: _____

_____

Your Words (Topic sentence with your opinion): _____

_____

_____

_____

_____

Research (Direct quote or paraphrase): _____

_____

_____

_____

_____

_____

Your Words (Analysis, summary, or transition): _____

_____

_____

_____

_____

SANDWICH WORKSHEET—TOPIC 2  RESEARCH

Topic Transistion:_____

_____

_____

_____

Your Words (Topic sentence with your opinion): _____

_____

_____

_____

_____

Research (Direct quote or paraphrase): _____

_____

_____

_____

_____

Your Words (Analysis, summary, or transition): _____

_____

_____

_____

_____

SANDWICH WORKSHEET—TOPIC 3 RESEARCH

Topic Transistion:_____

_____

_____

_____

Your Words (Topic sentence with your opinion): _____

_____

_____

_____

_____

Research (Direct quote or paraphrase): _____

_____

_____

_____

_____

Your Words (Analysis, summary, or transition): _____

_____

_____

_____

_____

SANDWICH WORKSHEET—TOPIC 4  RESEARCH

Topic Transistion:_____

_____

_____

_____

Your Words (Topic sentence with your opinion): _____

_____

_____

_____

_____

Research (Direct quote or paraphrase): _____

_____

_____

_____

_____

Your Words (Analysis, summary, or transition): _____

_____

_____

_____

_____

INTRODUCTIONS AND CONCLUSIONS

The introduction and conclusion are critical parts of your essay. The introduction is what grabs the reader's attention (or not!) and makes them want to read what you have to say. The conclusion is the last impression you will leave with the reader, and the last chance to persuade the reader to see your point of view.

INTRODUCTIONS

There are many ways to begin your paper, but the main consideration is to get the reader's attention. Sometimes your thesis statement works well enough on its own, but often you will want to start with some other type of attention-grabber before you state your thesis. Below are three ways to consider starting your essay, and an example of each. You can also see how your thesis statement might be adjusted to make the first paragraph flow smoothly.

Example Thesis: *Although researchers believe that the cause for eating disorders is complicated, media images are one of the main reasons girls develop these disorders.*

1. Anecdote

An anecdote is a short narrative, or story, that illustrates your point. This can be effective because the reader will want to know what happens next.

Example:

story   <u>My sister wanted to be a high-fashion model like the girls in the ads she ripped out of magazines and tacked to her wall. She was tall and beautiful, but she never felt she was thin enough. One day, after passing out in school, she was diagnosed with an eating disorder.</u> **Although** thesis

change

researchers believe that the cause for eating disorders is complicated, media images are one of the main reasons girls, like my sister, develop these disorders.

2. Interesting Information

A startling statistic or other tidbit of information that will shock or surprise your reader is a great attention-grabber.

Example:

information

thesis

change

Almost half of girls from fifth to twelfth grade want to lose weight because of magazine pictures, but only five percent of American females have the body type shown in most advertising (ANAD). Although researchers believe that the cause for eating disorders is complicated, given these statistics, it is easy to see that media images are one of the main reasons girls develop these disorders.

3. Overview

An overview engages readers by giving them a general idea of your topic and thesis, and an idea of one or more of the main points in the essay.

Example:

overview

thesis

Eating disorders are serious diseases that lead to death more often than any other mental illness. Although researchers believe that the cause for eating disorders is complicated, media images are one of the main reasons girls develop these disorders. When young girls are continually exposed to an ultra-thin ideal, they may begin unhealthy eating habits and develop poor self-esteem that leads to eating disorders.

CONCLUSIONS

Help! How do I end this thing? Sometimes the conclusion can be the hardest part of the essay. The worst thing you can do is just restate the introduction and/or thesis statement. The best thing you can do is to make sure that your conclusion flows naturally from your introduction. In short, it should be connected, not copied. If your introduction started with a story, tell the reader how it ended. If you started with a startling statistic, refer back to that information. If you used an overview, you might want to offer some sort of solution or thought-provoking idea.

Here are the previous introduction examples, along with conclusions that would work well with each.

INTRODUCTION #1:

My sister wanted to be a high-fashion model like the girls in the ads she ripped out of magazines and tacked to her wall. She was tall and beautiful, but she never felt she was thin enough. One day, after passing out in school, she was diagnosed with an eating disorder. Although researchers believe that the cause for eating disorders is complicated, media images are one of the main reasons girls, like my sister, develop these disorders.

CONCLUSION #1:

Fortunately, my sister received the help she needed and is recovering from her eating disorder. Many young girls, however, are still headed down the path of developing an eating disorder, until those that produce images in the media assume some responsibility for promoting an unachievable ideal.

INTRODUCTION #2:

Almost half of girls from fifth to twelfth grade want to lose weight because of magazine pictures, but only five percent of American females have the body type shown in most advertising (ANAD). Although researchers believe that the cause for eating disorders is complicated, given these statistics, it is easy to see that media images are one of the main reasons girls develop these disorders.

CONCLUSION #2:

If preteen and teen girls were regularly exposed to media images of women with average or varied body types instead of ultra-thin models, it is likely that not so many would develop eating disorders.

INTRODUCTION #3:

Eating disorders are serious diseases that lead to death more often than any other mental illness. Although researchers believe that the cause for eating disorders is complicated, media images are one of the main reasons girls develop these disorders. When young girls are continually exposed to an ultra-thin ideal, they may begin unhealthy eating habits and develop poor self-esteem that leads to eating disorders.

CONCLUSION #3:

Since eating disorders are potentially deadly for young women, the media must take some responsibility for their part in promoting these diseases by showing unrealistic images of an ideal body type. Consumers could be part of the solution by boycotting products that use these media images to sell their products. Until our society takes a stand against this unhealthy standard, young women will continue to be at risk.

ROUGH DRAFT

Now that you have your working thesis, research, and ideas for introductions and conclusions, you are ready to write a draft. This draft is meant to be a starting place, so don't worry about getting everything perfect. You will have plenty of time to revise and make improvements later.

After you have written the rough draft, follow these steps for revision:

1. Get at least two people to read your rough draft and critique it, using the Research Paper Critique Worksheet.

2. Complete the Next Step Worksheet.

After completing these steps, it is helpful to write another draft, revise, proofread, and then write your final draft.

RESEARCH PAPER CRITIQUE

Your name: _____

Author's name: _____

1. Underline the thesis statement. Does the thesis statement contain an opinion? Is it clear? Does it fit the scope of the paper? Give suggestions to make the thesis stronger.

_____

_____

_____

2. Does the introduction grab your attention? Why or why not?

_____

_____

_____

3. Is the essay logically organized? Does each paragraph have a topic sentence and stick to that topic? Mark any places where paragraphs go off-topic or where the paper seems unorganized.

_____

_____

_____

4. Identify at least two "research sandwiches" in the essay. Does the essay have a proper balance of research and the author's own opinions? Mark places on the essay where it needs more research or more of the author's own thoughts.

_____

_____

_____

5. Does the conclusion leave an effective last impression? Why or why not?

_____

_____

_____

6. Do the introduction and conclusion work well together? Why or why not?

_____

_____

_____

7. Note at least one thing the author has done well and one thing that needs improvement.

_____

_____

_____

NEXT STEP WORKSHEET

Name: _____

What are three things I learned about my essay from my critiques?

    1. _____

    2. _____

    3. _____

What two things do I need to do next to improve my essay? (List more if desired.)

    1. _____

    2. _____

RESEARCH PAPER GRADING RUBRIC

Introduction   /10 points

The essay grabs reader's attention, and is
interesting and relevant.

Thesis statement   /15 points

The thesis is clear, has an opinion, and fits
scope of paper.

Organization   /15 points

The essay is logically organized. Paragraphs
have topic sentences and clear transitions.

Research   /25 points

Outside sources are appropriate and
effectively integrated into the essay. There
is a proper balance of research and author
opinion.

Conclusion   /10 points

The conclusion is effective, not just a re-
statement of the thesis.

Conventions   /15 points

There are few errors in sentence structure,
grammar, spelling, and punctuation.

Citations /10 points

All outside sources are cited and the
citations are in the correct format. The works
cited page is included and in the proper
format.

————————————

100 points total

Comments:

CHAPTER SIX

ARGUMENTATIVE ESSAYS

An argumentative essay is much like a research paper, but it has a primary focus on convincing your reader to agree with you. You will broaden your argument to include counterclaims and rebuttals, and you will use the persuasive techniques of ethos, pathos, and logos to persuade your reader.

Use the writing prompts on page 124 for ideas, or choose your own topic. Whatever you choose, make sure it is something you care about. It is easier to be persuasive if you are passionate about your argument.

SAMPLE STUDENT ARGUMENTATIVE ESSAY

Peterson 1

Erik Peterson

Torres

English 100

30 April 2016

Ban Bottled Water

Americans spend billions of dollars every year on bottled water, and throw away billions of plastic water bottles, all while free, safe tap water is readily available. Not only is the cost and waste unnecessary, the increasing use of bottled water is creating a dire situation for the environment and may have hidden health risks for consumers. Although bottled water is a convenient product, it should be banned in areas where there is safe municipal drinking water because of the negative impact on the environment, animals, and public health.

Bottled water use negatively affects the environment in many ways. First, the production of plastic bottles is problematic. "It takes 15 million barrels of oil per year to make all of the plastic water bottles in America" (Knopper 38). This consumption of oil, along with the fuel used for transporting the water to stores, and then from stores to consumers' homes, is a waste of natural resources in the name of convenience. After the water is used, the impact on the environment becomes even more significant. Every second, Americans throw away 1,500 plastic bottles. At best, only 30 percent of bottles are recycled (Crane 18), meaning most plastic bottles end up in landfills. Of course, water is not the only beverage that is sold in plastic bottles, so critics might point out that even if bottled water is banned, consumers would buy other, less healthy beverages, and it limits consumer choice. Neither one of these scenarios has to be the case, as consumers could simply substitute a reusable container. Granted, this is sometimes not as convenient, but Americans can sacrifice a little bit of convenience for the sake preserving the environment.

Unfortunately, not all plastic bottles are recycled or even end up in landfills. A large number of plastic bottles end up washed into the ocean. According to marine scientist Marcus Eriksen, the total floating debris in the ocean is 500,000 tons (although other estimates put it as high as 200 million tons), and half of that is plastic bottles (Parker). The plastic is often ingested by animals. "The green and blue bottles, especially, look like tasty food to fish and shorebirds. Scientists are finding these dead animals on the beach, with bellies full of plastic pellets" (Knopper 38). The rate of plastic bottles in our ocean is continuously growing with the number of plastic bottles thrown away instead of recycled, so it is easy to see that the rate of dead animals filled with decayed plastic bottles is at a deadly rise. Who knows how long it will take for the ascending number of dead fish and animals to have a deadly blow on the overall, delicately balanced food chain? The effects may not be immediate, but it can be potentially deadly. The simple solution of recycling plastic bottles instead of throwing them away, however, is not realistic. In California, a recycling-friendly state, only 16 percent of plastic water bottles are recycled, with 1 billion going into the trash every year (Wilson et al.).

In addition to harming the environment and animals, bottled

water may also harm humans. Few people know that if bottled water is left in the light, algae or different types of bacteria can grow in the plastic water bottles. Furthermore, if bottled water gets warm, the plastic releases BPA, or bisphenol A. "In animal research, BPA and other endocrine disruptors have been linked to a range of unwanted effects—earlier puberty in females, enlarged prostates in males, and even cancer" (Claudio 201). How many people store water bottles in their car where they can be exposed to light and heat? "Bottled water should be stored in dark cool places. But most retailers, offices, and homeowners store their bottled water in open spaces where the water is exposed to light that can generate algae and bacteria growth in the water" (Malyk 1). Consequently, even if consumers store the water correctly, the damage may already be done.

Although it may be ideal that consumers of bottled water purchase the product as a healthier alternative to sugary soft drinks, people need to understand the risks, and also realize that what they are consuming may be simply tap water resold under a fancy label and packaged in a potentially toxic container. As an example, Nestlé has recently come under fire for bottling and reselling water from Sacramento's municipal water system during the state's epic drought (Davila). Of course, sometimes tap water can contain undesirable components, and some people do not like the taste, but there are other alternatives, such as home filtration systems and purchasing bottled water in larger containers that make less waste. Given these options, which can be used to fill reusable water bottles, there is no reason to purchase single serving plastic bottles.

The convenience of bottled water and its necessity in places where there is no clean drinking water available is indisputable, but the cost to the planet is too high for regular use among people who have access to free, clean, municipal drinking water. It is easy enough to fill a reusable water bottle rather than support a wasteful and dangerous industry. Some universities and cities around the United States have already banned bottled water, and this is a step in the right direction, but our entire population needs to get on board with banning bottled water to protect the future.

Works Cited

Crane, Cody. "NUTRITION: Bottled vs. Tap." *Scholastic Choice*, vol. 2, no. 3, 2011, p. 10, MasterFILE Premier, http://connection.ebscohost.com/c/articles/67719866/nutri-tion-bottled-vs-tap.

Davila, Robert. "Critics Take Aim at Nestlé Bottled Water Plant in Sacramento." *SacBee.com*, 25 April 2015, http://www.sacbee.com/news/investigations/the-public-eye/article19559868.html.

Knopper, Melissa. "Bottled Water Backlash." *E: The Environmental Magazine*, vol. 19, no. 3, 2008, p. 36. http://www.emagazine.com/author/guest/melissa-knopper/.

Parker, Laura. "The Best Way to Deal with Ocean Trash." *National Geographic*, 16 April 2014, http://news.nationalgeographic.com/news/2014/04/140414-ocean-garbage-patch-plastic-pacific-debris/.

Wilson, Ed, et al. "Report: Surge in Bottled Water Popularity Threatens Environment." Department of Conservation, 29 May 2003, CA.gov, http://www.conservation.ca.gov/index/news/2003%20News%20Releases/Pages/nr2003-13_wa-ter_bottle_crisis.aspx.

ARGUMENTATIVE ESSAY ASSIGNMENT

Write an argumentative essay about the topic of your choice. The purpose of the essay is to convince readers that your point of view is valid and logical. The essay should be 4–5 pages long (not including the Works Cited page), use at least 3 outside sources, and use MLA formatting. It should contain the following:

- An introduction.

- A thesis statement with a clearly defined argument on a relevant, debatable topic.

- Logical points of argument to support your claim.

- Evidence to support the points of your argument.

- Points of opposition and rebuttals.

- A conclusion.

The grading criteria is as follows:

Thesis 20 points
   The thesis statement is substantive and has a clearly defined argument.

Organization 25 points
   The essay is organized and supports the thesis with logical arguments.
   Clear and sufficient evidence, including appropriate outside sources, is present.

Counterclaims and Rebuttals 15 points
   Appropriate counterclaims and rebuttals are fair, present, and show a clear understanding of the topic and an awareness of the audience.

Introduction and Conclusion 15 points

The introduction and conclusion are engaging. The introduction provides an appropriate "hook." The conclusion reinforces the argument.

Writing Style 10 points

The writing is coherent, objective in tone, and contains appropriate transitions.

Conventions 15 points

The writer demonstrates command of grammar and punctuation.

The essay is in MLA format. All outside sources are cited appropriately.

Total 100 points

ARGUMENTATIVE ESSAY TIMELINE:

Topic Selection: Date Due: _____

Working Thesis: Date Due: _____

Research: Date Due: _____

Outline: Date Due: _____

Rough Draft: Date Due: _____

Final Essay: Date Due: _____

CHOOSING A TOPIC

Your choice of topic is the most important part of writing an argumentative essay. There are many things to consider when choosing your topic. It should be debatable, relevant, manageable, and supported with evidence.

DEBATABLE

Your topic must be something that allows for argument. If there are no differing viewpoints on the topic, then you haven't got an argument. For example, "It is difficult to live comfortably on minimum wage" is a statement that almost everyone would agree with.

"Minimum wage should be raised so every working American can afford a comfortable lifestyle" is debatable because not everyone would agree. Also, make sure your claim states the argument clearly. For example, "High speed police chases often put innocent people in danger" is a statement of fact that only implies an argument. A better claim would be "Police should not engage in high speed chases because they often put innocent people in danger."

RELEVANT

Avoid stale and obvious topics like the death penalty, abortion, gun control, or marijuana legalization. If you want to use one of these topics, be sure that you have a fresh, current take on it. For example, "Women should be able to have a legal abortion" is not a fresh debate. "Although protestors argue free speech, they should not be allowed to display graphic images outside of abortion clinics" is more interesting and current. To avoid using an overdone topic, look at what is in the news today. Is your city or state considering raising the minimum wage? Are there interesting propositions coming up in an election? Is your school considering requiring uniforms? Watch the news or look at some online news sites. What piques your interest?

MANAGEABLE

The narrower your topic, the easier it will be to write a short essay. With only a few pages, writing effectively about the problems with health care reform would be impossible. Focusing on one or two problems associated with heath care reform would be more manageable. If you are starting with a broad topic that is interesting to you, such as genetically modified foods, you can make a list of questions or issues about the topic after doing a bit of research, then choose a particular focus, such as whether labeling of genetically modified foods should be required.

SUPPORTED WITH EVIDENCE

Make sure that your topic can be supported with evidence. Arguing an issue from a moral standpoint can be problematic because logical evidence might be hard to find. For example, finding evidence for the claim "Laws that prohibit physician-assisted suicide are wrong" is more difficult to support than "Physician-assisted suicide should be legal so that patient choice is not limited." Although you want a narrow, focused topic, if you go too far in this direction, you might limit the evidence you can find. For example, if you want to argue that building a local bike trail is worth the taxpayer dollars, it might be hard to find definitive evidence for that particular trail. If you expand your argument to show that bike trails in local communities in general increase residents' satisfaction and promote fitness, then you can apply that to your local argument.

CHOOSING A TOPIC

Name: _____

Write down three topic ideas:

1. _____

2. _____

3. _____

1. Choose one topic and free write for five minutes. Don't worry about grammar, punctuation, or complete sentences. Don't pause in your writing or stop to think; keep writing as fast as you can. Keep the following questions in mind as you write: What do I already know about it? Why is it important to me? What do I think about it? Why would it matter to other people? What are other opinions about the topic?

2. Repeat this for each remaining topic.

3. After completing the exercise, answer the following questions:

Which topic was the easiest to write about?

_____

Which topic did I want to learn more about?

_____

Which topic did I find the most interesting?

_____

Which topic did I have the strongest opinion about?

_____

Which topic might be most interesting for my audience?

_____

After answering the questions above, choose one topic and do another five-minute free write, this time starting with your opinion on the topic.

EXAMPLE NARROWING YOUR TOPIC WORKSHEET

Start with your topic at the top of the triangle. Write two more versions, each narrower than the previous one, both in scope and specific language.

childhood vaccinations should be required.

Parents should be required to get their children vaccinated before school.

Parents should be required by law to have their children vaccinated before their children are allowed to attend public or private school.

NARROWING YOUR TOPIC WORKSHEET

Name: _____

Start with your topic at the top of the triangle. Write two more versions, each narrower than the previous one, both in scope and specific language.

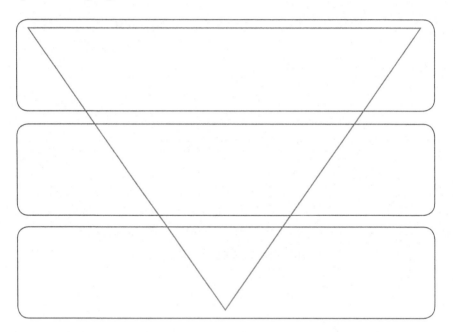

DETERMINING PURPOSE

The purpose of an argumentative essay, besides presenting a solid argument, is to persuade readers to do something. It's important to determine what that something is before you write the essay. The purpose can be to solve a problem, present a plan of action, or simply to get the readers to agree with your opinion. This purpose may or may not be included in your thesis, but the paper should be making a case for it as it progresses. It is also an excellent starting point for your conclusion. Here are some examples of the three purposes, using the topic of the cost of college:

PROBLEM SOLVING:

Once a student has been accepted to a college, the tuition should be capped at the rate when he or she entered, to prevent unexpected increases that the student may not be able to afford.

PLAN OF ACTION:

Voters should vote "Yes" on Proposition 42, which raises funds through sales tax to help keep the cost of tuition down for students enrolled in the state's public colleges.

AGREEMENT:

The rising cost of tuition at four-year universities should cause students to assess whether the debt they will accumulate makes sense compared to the worth of their degree.

Use your own topic to try out each purpose and see which is the best fit for your essay:

Problem Solving: _____

Plan of Action: _____

Agreement: _____

ADDRESSING THE OPPOSITION

Addressing the opposition's viewpoint is a necessary part of creating a solid argument. There are several reasons you should bring up the counterpoints to your arguments.

- It shows that you are knowledgeable about the topic. If you ignore alternate viewpoints, you will seem uninformed about the topic, and you will lose your reader's trust that you have done your research and carefully thought through each point.

- You can strengthen your own arguments by refuting or diminishing opposing points. It gives you an opportunity to fully persuade your audience.

- Demonstrating that you have researched opposing arguments shows that you are not biased and have given all the information consideration. You will seem more fair and balanced in your arguments.

Use the Pros and Cons Worksheet to list all the points and opposing points you can think of for your topic. This will give you a starting point on what to research.

PRoS AND CONS WORKSHEET

Topic:	
Pros	Cons
Circle the top reasons that support your argument. These will become topic sentences in the body paragraphs of your essay.	Circle the top reasons that oppose your argument. You will want to address these in the body paragraphs of your essay.

CREATING A WORKING THESIS

The thesis statement is the most important part of the argumentative essay. It states your position and sets expectations for what will follow in the essay. A "working thesis" is basically your thesis rough draft. You need to have a direction before you begin your paper, but as you write and research, you may find that you want to revise your thesis.

One way to create a working thesis statement is to use the "Opposition-Opinion-Reason" template. Using this method, you address the main point of opposition to your stance, state your opinion, and give the main reason why you hold this opinion. Whether or not you end up using the thesis in this format for the final draft, it's a good exercise to clarify your idea.

Examples

Although standardized testing in schools is only one measure of students' learning [Opposition], it is the fairest way to assess student learning [Opinion] because other methods tend to be subjective. [Reason]

Some children respond well to medications for ADD and ADHD [Opposition], but they are overprescribed [Opinion] because parents and teachers are often unaware of, or unwilling to try, alternative treatments. [Reason]

Try writing your topic into this format:

What Makes a Good Thesis Statement?

1. It has a clearly defined argument.

   Poor: An issue that has been debated lately is whether genetically modified foods should be labeled.

   Poor: In this paper, I will discuss the pros and cons of requiring manufacturers to label genetically modified foods.

   Good: All products that contain genetically modified foods should be labeled.

2. It contains one main idea.

   Poor: College student athletes should not be paid to participate in sports because they are already compensated through scholarships, and it is not fair to other groups of students, such as veterans, who should have easier access to financial aid.

   Poor: Paying college student athletes for their participation in sports will put the focus even more on the sport rather than academics for these students, and some athletes should not even be admitted to the school in the first place because they do not have the same qualifications as the rest of the students.

   Good: College student athletes should not be paid for their participation in sports because it would create an environment where the paycheck for playing would become more important than academics, which should be their primary focus.

3. It uses specific terms.

   Poor: Police should not be recording.

   Poor: Police should not be recording with cameras because it invades privacy.

Good: Police should not be required to wear body cameras when interacting with citizens because the cameras create privacy issues, such as when police enter private residences.

4. It is interesting and engaging (avoids the "so-what" problem).
   Poor: There are advantages and disadvantages to starting college immediately after high school.
   Poor: Some people think students should work or volunteer for a year before starting college.
   Good: Working or volunteering for a year after high school before starting college leads to greater success in academics and future earnings.

5. It can be supported by research.
   Poor: Photoshopped media images cause eating disorders.
   Poor: Images of photoshopped models cause all girls to feel bad about their bodies, leading to eating disorders.
   Good: Images of ultra-thin, photoshopped models are a contributing factor to eating disorders in young women.

TIPS

- Make sure your thesis fits the scope of your paper. If you have two or three pages, you'll want a narrow topic that you can cover adequately.
- Do not start your thesis statement with "I believe . . ." or "In my opinion . . ."
- Do not "announce" your topic, for example, "In this paper I will be discussing . . ."
- Make sure your thesis is not just a statement of fact, (for example, "An eating disorder is a serious illness") but contains your opinion.

THESIS WORKSHEET

Name: _____

Working Thesis: _____

Answer YES or NO to the following questions:

Does my thesis have a clearly defined argument?
Does my thesis contain one main idea?
Does my thesis contain specific terms?
Is my thesis interesting and engaging?
Can my thesis be supported by research?
Can I adequately cover the subject in the pages given?

Rewrite your thesis here. Make sure you do not use phrases such as "In my opinion . . . " or "I believe . . . "

Revised Thesis:

TYPES OF ARGUMENTS AND EVIDENCE

For each reason you give to support your thesis statement, you will need to argue it logically and give evidence to support your claim.

Here are some examples of logical argument types on the topic of e-cigarettes:

- **Give relevant examples**

  E-cigarette manufacturers inappropriately market their product to teens by, for example, selling them in malls and online, producing them in flavors that appeal to young people, and leaving them devoid of any warning labels.

- **Present a comparison or a contrast**

  The only benefit of e-cigarettes is that they are a tool to help people stop smoking conventional cigarettes, but since studies show that a nicotine inhaler is just as effective (Bullen et al., 102), there is no reason that e-cigarettes should be widely available.

- **Show a cause-and-effect relationship**

  Teens who use e-cigarettes are likely to become conventional smokers. CDC Director Tom Frieden said, "Nicotine is a highly addictive drug. Many teens who start with e-cigarettes may be condemned to struggling with a lifelong addiction to nicotine and conventional cigarettes" (qtd. in Chan).

- **Argue by definition**

  E-cigarettes are not a safe or benign alternative to conventional cigarettes. They may have less nicotine and fewer chemicals, but they share the fundamental purpose of conventional cigarettes: inhaling highly addictive nicotine.

In general, the majority of your evidence should come from academic sources, but there are some other types of evidence that can be effective.

Here are some examples:

- **Personal experience**

  At a party I attended recently, several friends who had never touched a conventional cigarette didn't think twice about trying e-cigarettes that were being passed around, reassured by others that they were "safe" and "not addictive."

- **Primary source material** (interview/survey/questionnaire)

  A poll of 50 of my classmates at Hoover High School showed that 75% of them do not believe e-cigarettes contain nicotine.

- **Hypothetical example**

  A teen might think she is being safe by using e-cigarettes instead of conventional cigarettes, but she could easily become addicted to the nicotine in most e-cigarettes, and even experience withdrawal symptoms. She could then become addicted to cigarettes as an adult, as her addiction gets worse.

- **Graphics**

  Graphics come from academic source material, but can be a more effective way to make a point than words alone.

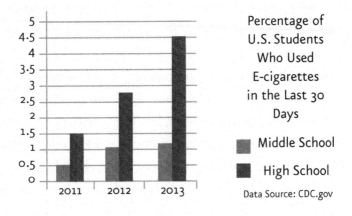

Percentage of U.S. Students Who Used E-cigarettes in the Last 30 Days

Middle School

High School

Data Source: CDC.gov

DEFENDING YOUR ARGUMENT

Once you have made your argument and showed evidence to back it, you will want to address the opposition, or counterpoint, with a rebuttal to further strengthen your argument. Below are some effective strategies and examples.

- **Show that the counterpoint is illogical, or that the underlying assumption is incorrect.**

  Argument: The minimum wage should not be raised to $15.00 per hour.

  Counterpoint: Every worker should make enough money to live above the poverty line.

  Rebuttal: Many minimum wage jobs serve workers who are not trying to make a full-time living and support a family. Raising the minimum wage to $15.00 an hour will eliminate entry-level jobs for unskilled workers or young people who do not need to make a full-time living, such as high school and college students.

- **Show that the counterpoint has merit, but does not show the whole picture.**

  Argument: Companies cannot afford the cost of raising the minimum wage to $15.00 per hour.

  Counterpoint: Companies can absorb the extra cost of raising the minimum wage or pass the extra cost along to consumers.

  Rebuttal: It is true that companies could find ways to absorb or pass along the cost to consumers if the minimum wage increase were the only factor, but there are other, hidden costs. For example, if an experienced worker currently makes $15.00 an hour and the employer is forced to hire inexperienced workers for $15.00 per hour, the employer will have to raise the pay of the experienced worker because he or she will no longer be happy earning minimum wage after years of hard work and with a superior skill set.

- **Show the counterpoint is not relevant, or has little impact.**
  Argument: Raising the minimum wage to $15.00 an hour will force employers to hire less people and consolidate jobs.
  Counterpoint: Even if employers cut workers' hours, the workers will still come away with more money since they are earning higher wages.
  Rebuttal: Less hours for higher wage sounds appealing, but jobs will be harder to find, and workloads will be higher as jobs are consolidated.

- **Show the counterpoint has merit, but does not supersede the other points.**
  Argument: Companies should not be forced to inflate the value of unskilled workers.
  Counterpoint: Companies are greedy and will keep wages as low as they can to take advantage of workers.
  Rebuttal: It is true that labor laws and a base minimum wage are necessary to keep unethical companies in check, but overall, market forces will determine what a worker's skill set is worth. Only a small percentage of jobs in the United States are paid at minimum wage. Instead of lobbying a company to inflate the worth of a minimum wage job, workers should seek to improve their situations through education so their labor is worth more to employers.

ARGUMENT ORGANIZER

Here is a chart to help you organize your arguments, counterpoints, and rebuttals.

Name:		
Point	Counterpoint	Rebuttal

OUTLINES

There is no one correct way to organize your essay, but the following outline templates offer two good ways to organize your paper. Try them both to see which is the best fit for your topic.

OUTLINE TEMPLATE # 1

Name: _____

Introduction: _____

Thesis: _____

Claim #1 (Topic Sentence): _____

    Evidence: _____

    Counterclaim: _____

    Rebuttal: _____

Claim #2 (Topic Sentence): _____

    Evidence: _____

    Counterclaim: _____

    Rebuttal: _____

Claim #3 (Topic Sentence): _____

    Evidence: _____

    Counterclaim: _____

    Rebuttal: _____

Conclusion: _____

OUTLINE TEMPLATE #2

Name: _____

Introduction: _____

Thesis: _____

Claim #1 (Topic Sentence): _____

    Evidence: _____

    Concluding sentence: _____

Claim #2 (Topic Sentence): _____

    Evidence: _____

    Concluding sentence: _____

Claim #3 (Topic Sentence): _____

    Evidence: _____

    Concluding sentence: _____

Counterpoint #1: _____

    Rebuttal: _____

Counterpoint #2: _____

    Rebuttal: _____

Conclusion: _____

TRANSITIONS

Effective transitions are an important part of any writing, but they are particularly important in argumentative writing, as you are moving between your opinions, points, counterpoints, and rebuttals. To keep your writing clear and flowing seamlessly between ideas, good transitions are key. Here is an example of two body paragraphs that use effective transitions:

In addition to harming the environment and animals, bottled water may also harm humans. Few people know that if bottled water is left in the light, algae or different types of bacteria can grow in the plastic water bottles. **Furthermore,** if bottled water gets warm, the plastic releases BPA, or bisphenol A. "In animal research, BPA and other endocrine disruptors have been linked to a range of unwanted effects—earlier puberty in females, enlarged prostates in males, and even cancer" (Claudio 201). How many people store water bottles in their car where they can be exposed to light and heat? "Bottled water should be stored in dark cool places. Most retailers, offices, and homeowners store their bottled water in open spaces where the water is exposed to light that can generate algae and bacteria growth in the water" (Malyk 1). **Consequently,** even if consumers store the water correctly, the damage may already be done.

Although it may be ideal that consumers of bottled water purchase the product as a healthier alternative to sugary soft drinks, people need to understand the risks, and also realize that what they are consuming may be simply tap water resold under a fancy label and packaged in a potentially toxic container. **As an example,** Nestlé has recently come under fire for bottling and reselling water from Sacramento's municipal water system during the state's epic drought (Davila). **Of course**, sometimes tap water can contain undesirable components, and some people do not like the taste, but there are other alternatives, such as home filtration systems and purchasing bottled water in larger containers that make less waste. **Given these options,** which can be used to fill reusable water bottles, there is no reason to purchase single serving plastic bottles.

TRANSITIONS LIST

ADDITION/EXAMPLE

For example, for instance, specifically, in fact, namely, in other words, to illustrate, especially, such as, similarly, in addition to, equally important, likewise, in the same way, furthermore, moreover, therefore, thus, as well as, in like manner, by the same token

COMPARE

Likewise, in similar fashion, in addition to, in a like manner, analogous to, as much as, as well as, for example, similarly, another, to put it another way, namely

CONTRAST

On the contrary, however, while this may be true, nevertheless, at the same time, unless, on the other hand, in contrast, in spite of, conversely, be that as it may, even though, regardless, otherwise, even though, then again

CONCLUSIONS

Therefore, consequently, accordingly, on the whole, generally speaking, all things considered, in the long run, given these points, on balance, obviously, ultimately

CHRONOLOGICAL ORDER

Subsequently, immediately, rarely, usually, afterward, before, formerly, finally, at the same time, meanwhile, previously, concurrently, simultaneously, in the mean time, in the first place, to begin with, in due time, presently, eventually

CAUSE AND EFFECT

In the event that, with this in mind, for fear that, in order to, for the purpose of, on the condition that, due to, because of, as a result, consequently, therefore

CONSEQUENCE

Consequently, accordingly, for this reason, as a result, in spite of, due to, so that, for this reason, under those circumstances

EMPHASIS

Above all, of course, surely, in fact, to clarify, that is to say, to put it another way, a key point, a point often overlooked, indeed, certainly, especially, particularly, most important, even greater, primarily, above all, surprisingly, obviously, without a doubt

INTRODUCTIONS

The introduction to your essay should accomplish two things. First, it needs to "hook" your readers, meaning it catches their attention so they want to keep reading. Second, it should logically set up your thesis statement. You only get one first impression, so it's best to think about how to begin your paper carefully. A typical introduction will end with the thesis statement. There are many approaches to engaging introductions. Here are a few:

- **Personal experience**

  I used e-cigarettes for one month last year, thinking they were perfectly safe. I was surprised that when I quit using them, I had nicotine withdrawal symptoms such as insomnia, headaches, and cravings.

- **Shocking or interesting fact or statistic**

  According to the Centers for Disease Control, the number of teens using e-cigarettes in 2014 tripled from the previous year.

- **Relevant story or anecdote**

  Teens interviewed by *The New York Times* say the reasons they started using e-cigarettes vary, from wanting something that was "edgy and "exciting" at 13 years old, to using them to stop smoking regular cigarettes at 18. Joe Stevonson says he prefers a flavor endorsed by rapper Lil Ugly Mane called Courtroom. The flavor is touted as "a medley of things you might want while waiting for the jury to convict" (Tavernise).

- **Compare and contrast**

  Although cigarette use among teenagers is continuing on its downward trend, use of e-cigarettes is skyrocketing.

- **Analogy**

  According to many in the e-cigarette community, conventional cigarettes are to e-cigarettes what a horse and buggy is to a modern car.

- **Quote from a relevant source, famous person, or historical figure**

  Dr. Vivek Murthy, U.S. Surgeon General, recently said, "I'm concerned about e-cigarettes, and I think this is an area where we are in desperate need of clarity" (AP).

- **Debunk a myth**

  Contrary to popular belief, most e-cigarettes are not free from harmful chemicals.

- **Prediction**

  Given the exponential growth of e-cigarettes among teens and how little is known about the long-term effects, the United States is facing a health care time bomb.

CONCLUSIONS

The conclusion is your last chance to make a convincing argument to your readers, so make it count. Although the conclusion should remind the reader of your thesis, it should not be a repeat or a simple rewording, but bring the paper to a satisfying ending. If the purpose of your paper was to solve a problem or serve as a call to action, the conclusion is the perfect place to state this implicitly. Here are some strategies and brief examples.

- **Call to action**

  Citizens should support legislation that requires labeling and regulation of e-cigarettes and should petition lawmakers to limit marketing toward young people.

- **Show the greater implications of your argument**
Given the exponential rise in the use of e-cigarettes among young people, and the misconception that they are a safe alternative to conventional cigarettes, the United States could be facing a problem in the near future as big as or bigger than cigarette smoking at its height.

- **Warning**
Little is known about the long-term effects of e-cigarette usage, but they have been shown to be addictive, contain harmful chemicals, and even lead to smoking conventional cigarettes. Young people who use e-cigarettes will inevitably face addiction and other health issues.

- **Circle back to the introduction**
Luckily, I was able to see for myself, by weathering the nicotine withdrawal, that e-cigarettes are not the benign fun my friends made them out to be.

- **Quote from a relevant source, famous person, or historical figure**
As the Irish Minster for Health said, "Less toxic does not mean more healthy for me" (EPSCO Press Conference).

- **Rhetorical Question**
How can teens be aware of the health risks of e-cigarettes when the products are not labeled, are barely regulated by the FDA, and are marketed directly to them?

CONDUCTING RESEARCH

For an argumentative essay, you will want to read as much on your topic as you can, and then select a few good sources to use in your essay. It is important that your sources are qualified academic sources. Review the material on pages 72–73 to make sure you are using appropriate sources.

It is helpful to take notes on your sources, or print them out and annotate them (see pages 106–107 for a review on annotating). You can also use the Source Worksheet to record your notes and keep track of the publication information for citations.

SOURCE WORKSHEET

Name: _____

Authors: _____

Title: _____

Source (website, journal, magazine, book): _____

Volume/Issue: _____

Publisher: _____

Page numbers: _____

Medium (web, print, DVD, personal interview): _____

Date of access (if online): _____

Summary of source: _____

_____

_____

_____

Notes and quotes: _____

_____

_____

_____

_____

_____

_____

_____

_____

_____

_____

PERSUASIVE TECHNIQUES

Ethos, pathos, and *logos* are three persuasive techniques you can use to convince your audience to agree with you. If you can use all of these techniques in your essay, you have a better chance of your audience responding to your ideas favorably.

ETHOS

Ethos is the Greek word for "character." In order to convince people to agree with you, you need to establish that you are worth listening to. If your audience thinks you are trustworthy, knowledge-able, likeable, and respectable, they will tend to believe what you are saying. The impression you make on the reader is just as important as the information you present.

In an essay, you can persuade your reader with *ethos* by your tone (fair, professional, pleasant), by addressing the opposition respectfully (showing you understand what people who hold different opinions care about), by sharing a relevant personal experience, and by presenting an error-free, well-written, organized paper.

Example: While it is understandable that some parents are wary of getting their children immunized due to occasional adverse side effects, watching my sister suffer from measles and the subsequent complications convinced me at a young age that immunizations are worth the small risk.

PATHOS

Pathos means appealing to the audience's emotions. If you can inspire an emotional connection with your audience (get them to feel what you feel, such as anger or pity, or get them to feel sympathetic to your cause), they are more likely to agree with your position.

Pathos is accomplished in an essay by presenting facts that engage your audience's emotions, or by presenting stories or hypothetical situations that people can relate to on an emotional level.

Example: For forty-nine people, including young children, a Disneyland vacation turned into a nightmare when they contracted measles, an entirely preventable disease through immunizations, at the Happiest Place on Earth.

LOGOS

Logos means to persuade an audience by logic. This is where you present facts, evidence, and reason to convince your audience.

Citing authorities, using logical arguments and rebuttals, and showing that your argument is well-researched, are examples of *logos* in your essay.

Example: Although many parents are concerned about the link between autism and vaccinations, the original study that created this alarm has been retracted. In addition, in response to the concerns that stemmed from the faulty study, the ingredient in question, Thimerosal, has been almost entirely removed from vaccinations since 2001 (Harris 3).

ETHOS, PATHOS, AND LOGOS WORKSHEET

Name: _____

Choose one of your arguments, and explore one way you can incorporate *ethos*, *pathos*, and *logos* to strengthen your argument.

Argument:
Ethos
Pathos
Logos

LOGICAL FALLACIES

Your arguments need to be logical in order to be convincing. You will lose credibility if the reader can poke your argument full of holes. Below are examples of errors in logic that you will want to avoid.

- **Generalizations:** "Children no longer play outside and interact with others; they are at home, glued to their electronics." This may be true for some children, but it is certainly not true for all, so this is not a valid statement.

- **Faulty analogy:** "Using bottled water should be regarded by society as irresponsible, just like smoking while pregnant." These two things are so dissimilar, the comparison doesn't work. It causes the reader to think, "What?" instead of making a solid point.

- **Straw man (misrepresenting the real argument or focusing on an irrelevant point as a distraction from the real issue):** "People who want to cut the budget for food stamps don't care if children go to bed hungry at night." Certainly no one wants children to go to bed hungry at night, so this is a point that is not relevant to the argument.

- **Bandwagon appeal (implies that everyone else agrees with your argument):** "Everyone knows that organic food is better than non-organic food." Instead of trying to convince the reader that organic food is better through facts, the writer implies that the reader has an unacceptable opinion if he or she does not believe this.

- **False Dilemma:** "If energy drinks are not banned, young people will continue to suffer dangerous health consequences." This argument assumes there is only choice, rather than multiple possibilities. Energy drinks could be regulated, be made illegal for minors, or be required to reduce or eliminate certain ingredients, et cetera.

- **Quick fix:** "Parents should control their children so they will not become criminals." This is a simplistic statement. It doesn't have any practical application and skirts the more complicated issues of why kids become criminals.

- **Red herring (distraction from the real issue):** "The fracking operation may be dangerous for the environment, but if it is shut down, what will happen to the workers who depend on it for their living?" By bringing up the emotional topic of workers losing their jobs, the writer avoids the real issue of the problem of fracking.

- **Ad hominem (attack on character rather than the issue):** "Anyone who supports the zoning allowance of marijuana dispensaries near residential neighborhoods has a drug-addled brain." This argument attacks the character of people with a different opinion rather than sticking to the argument.

- **Ad populum (assuming an argument is correct because it is popular):** "Bacon cheeseburgers are the students' favorite food, so they should be added to the lunch menu." This argument assumes that just because something is popular means that it is correct or valid.

- **Non sequitur ("it doesn't follow"):** "If the school board was made up of parents instead of administrators, the schools would be run more efficiently." This conclusion does not follow the premise because it's not necessarily true that parents would be more efficient than administrators.

LOGICAL FALLACIES EXERCISE

Note the type of logical fallacy each sentence represents, then explain why the logic is faulty.

1. Anyone who agrees that the current school system is adequate doesn't care about children learning to read and write.

2. Three quarters of the students voted to change the rules to allow students to leave the campus whenever they want, so the administration should get rid of the lock on the parking lot gate.

3. If college was free for everyone, there would be no poverty because college graduates earn more money.

4. Every patriotic American will vote for the candidate that wants to increase military spending.

5. Teens are addicted to their phones; they can't be without them for even a few hours.

6. The minimum wage should not be raised to $15.00 an hour. My grandpa made that much money in a week when he was twenty, and he never complained.

7. The parents of college students who want to repeal privacy laws so they can see their children's grades and attendance are overprotective and want to interfere where they don't belong.

8. Drinking unhealthy beverages such as soda is just as irresponsible as someone driving with his or her eyes closed.

9. If the size of sodas is not regulated, the rate of people with diabetes will continue to soar.

10. People on welfare should get jobs so we can cut spending.

LOGICAL FALLACIES EXERCISE ANSWER KEY

1. Anyone who agrees that the current school system is adequate doesn't care about children learning to read and write. **Straw Man: Agreeing that the current school system is adequate does not mean that a person doesn't care if children are illiterate.**

2. Three quarters of the students voted to change the rules to allow students to leave the campus whenever they want, so the administration should get rid of the lock on the parking lot gate. **Ad Populum: This argument assumes that just because something is popular, it must be correct, and therefore, the school administration should act on it.**

3. If college was free for everyone, there would be no poverty because college graduates earn more money. **Non Sequitur: It is not necessarily true that a college education eliminates poverty, nor would everyone necessarily attend college or earn more money afterwards.**

4. Every patriotic American will vote for the candidate that wants to increase military spending. **Bandwagon Appeal: Instead of trying to convince the reader that increased military spending is good for the country, the writer implies that the reader is not patriotic if he or she does not believe this.**

5. Teens are addicted to their phones; they can't be without them for even a few hours. **Generalization: This may be true for some teens, but it is certainly not true for all, so this is not a valid statement.**

6. The minimum wage should not be raised to $15.00 an hour. My grandpa made that much money in a week when he was twenty, and he never complained.
   Red Herring: There is little relevancy in how much a grandparent made many decades ago to the current wage issue. Grandpa's stoic attitude is a diversion from the real issue of whether or not the minimum wage should be raised.

7. The parents of college students who want to repeal privacy laws so they can see their children's grades and attendance are overprotective and want to interfere where they don't belong.
   Ad Hominem: This argument attacks the character of the parents rather than sticking to the argument.

8. Drinking unhealthy beverages such as soda is just as irresponsible as someone driving with his or her eyes closed.
   Faulty Analogy: These two things are so dissimilar, the comparison doesn't work. It causes the reader to think, "What?" instead of making a solid point.

9. If the size of sodas is not regulated, the rate of people with diabetes will continue to soar.
   False Dilemma: This argument assumes there is only one factor in the diabetes rate, and only one solution. There are multiple causes and multiple ways to approach the problem.

10. People on welfare should get jobs so we can cut spending.
    Quick Fix: This is a simplistic statement. It doesn't have any practical application and skirts the more complicated issues of why people are on welfare.

ROUGH DRAFT

Now that you have a thesis, your research, and an outline, you are ready to write a draft. This draft is meant to be a starting place, so don't worry about getting everything perfect. You will have plenty of time to revise and make improvements later.

After you have your rough draft, do the following steps to revise:

1. Get at least two people to read your rough draft and critique it, using the Argumentative Essay Critique Worksheet.

2. Complete the Next Step Worksheet.

After completing these steps, it is helpful to write another draft, revise, proofread, and then write your final draft.

ARGUMENTATIVE ESSAY CRITIQUE

Your Name: _____

Author's Name: _____

1. Is the introduction interesting? Did it make you want to keep reading?

2. Is the author's opinion clear? Is there a clearly defined argument?

3. Does each paragraph of the essay contain a clear point that supports the main argument?

4. Is there evidence to support each point?

5. Are the opposing points of view addressed sufficiently?

6. Are the rebuttals to the opposing points sufficient and logical?

7. Are there any logical fallacies?

8. Is the essay organized in a logical way?

9. Does the writing flow smoothly? Are there appropriate transitions?

10. Is the conclusion logical?

11. Does the conclusion provide a satisfying ending to the paper?

12. What are three things the author did well?

   1.

   2.

   3.

13. What are three things that need improvement?

   1.

   2.

   3.

NEXT STEP WORKSHEET

Name: _____

What are three things I learned about my essay from my critiques?

1. _____

2. _____

3. _____

What two things do I need to do next to improve my essay? (List more if desired.)

1. _____

2. _____

3. _____

Plan of action to improve my essay:

GRADING RUBRIC

Thesis   /20 points

The thesis statement is substantive and has a
clearly defined argument.

Organization   /25 points

The essay is organized and supports the
thesis with logical arguments.
Clear and sufficient evidence, including
appropriate outside sources, is present.

Counterclaims and Rebuttals   /15 points

There are appropriate counterclaims, and
rebuttals are fair, present, and show a clear
understanding of the topic and an awareness
of the audience.

Introduction and Conclusion   /15 points

The introduction and conclusion are
engaging. The introduction provides
an appropriate "hook." The conclusion
reinforces the argument.

Writing Style   /10 points

The writing is coherent, objective in tone,
and contains appropriate transitions.

Conventions   /15 points

The writer demonstrates a command of
grammar and punctuation.
The essay is in MLA format. All outside
sources are cited appropriately.

_____

/100 points total

Comments:

CHAPTER SEVEN

WRITING PROMPTS

Would American workers be happier and more productive if the 40-hour work week were reduced?

Should men get the same amount of time off for paternity leave as women get for maternity leave?

Should advertisers be banned from advertising unhealthy foods directly to children?

How much responsibility does the fast food industry have for the childhood obesity problem?

Should food manufacturers be required to label products that contain genetically modified foods?

Are people overly reliant on their phones and computers?

Should the United States make English the national language?

Is the minimum wage fair? Should it be raised to provide a comfortable standard of living for a full-time worker?

Should police officers wear cameras?

Should zoos and animal parks be phased out?

Should financial aid for college be based on merit, need, or both?

What kind of penalties should be imposed for athletes who are caught doping?

Should students be paid for good grades? Should there be incentives from parents to do well in school?

Why don't most diets work?

Is sex education in schools effective or necessary?

Should doctors be allowed to participate in assisted suicide?

What responsibility do school administrators have for student bullying? On campus? Off campus? On social media?

Should college admissions representatives consider social media postings in their decisions? What about employers or landlords?

Do photoshopped images contribute to low self-esteem? Are they a factor in eating disorders? Should they be labeled or regulated?

Should citizens of the United States give up privacies in the interest of national security? Should the government let citizens know when these privacies are violated (such as monitoring phone calls or emails)?

Would a flat tax be more fair than the current tax code?

Should famous people be entitled to more privacy? What about their children and other family members?

Should there be age limits on children participating in contact sports such as football?

Should schools provide breakfast and lunch to all students? Should schools provide meals during school breaks?

ABOUT THE AUTHOR

Laura Torres is the author and editor of many books for young people. She currently teaches first-year college composition, writes curriculum for K–12, and writes a blog for secondary teachers at compositionclassroom.blogspot.com. She holds a BA and MA in English.

ABOUT FAMILIUS

VISIT OUR WEBSITE: WWW.FAMILIUS.COM

JOIN OUR FAMILY

There are lots of ways to connect with us! Subscribe to our news-letters at www.familius.com to receive uplifting daily inspiration, essays from our Pater Familius, a free ebook every month, and the first word on special discounts and Familius news.

GET BULK DISCOUNTS

If you feel a few friends and family might benefit from what you've read, let us know and we'll be happy to provide you with quantity discounts. Simply email us at orders@familius.com.

CONNECT

Facebook: www.facebook.com/paterfamilius
Twitter: @familiustalk, @paterfamilius1
Pinterest: www.pinterest.com/familius
Instagram: @familiustalk

FAMILIUS

THE MOST IMPORTANT WORK YOU EVER DO WILL BE
WITHIN THE WALLS OF YOUR OWN HOME.